THE WEATHER

MERVYN LINFORD

THE LITTORAL PRESS

First Published 2005

The Littoral Press
38 Barringtons, 10 Sutton Rd.
Southend-on-Sea, Essex SS2 5NA
United Kingdom

British Library Cataloguing-in-Publication Data:
A catalogue record of this book is available from
The British Library

ISBN 978-09541844-8-3

Printed by 4edge Ltd. Hockley, Essex

CONTENTS

January	5
February	16
March	27
April	38
May	49
June	61
July	72
August	84
September	95
October	107
November	120
December	132

'With all the intensity of feeling which exalted me, all the intense communion I held with the earth, the sun and the sky, the stars hidden by the light, with the ocean - in no manner can the thrilling depth of these feelings be written - with these I prayed, as if they were the keys of an instrument, of an organ, with which I swelled forth the notes of my soul, redoubling my own voice by their power.'

Time has never existed, and never will; it is a purely artificial arrangement. It is eternity now, it always was eternity, and always will be. By no possible means could I get into time if I tried. I am in eternity now and must there remain. Haste not, be at rest, this Now is eternity.'

Two quotes from 'The Story of my Heart' an autobiography - Richard Jefferies - 1848-1887.

'Were we led all that way for Birth or Death? There was a Birth, certainly, we had evidence and no doubt. I had seen birth and death, but had thought they were different; this Birth was hard and bitter agony for us, like Death, our death.'

Journey of the Magi - T S Eliot - 1888-1965

JANUARY

Contrast

The contrast of the blackbirds in the snow
Is something that composes in the mind -
An icy thought. Of people long ago

Through fields of white - who trudge the bitter edge
Of all they know and feel the bite of hunger -
Far from home. The hunters through the hedgerows

And the heath - who pray to gods unnumbered
In the cold - to warm their flesh. What pledges
Can the deities still keep - when under

Frost's dominion they patrol the moment
That is ghosted on their breath? The thought's defined
At last. Blackbirds in the branches strike a pose -

Reminding us through windows in the sun
That winter - comes between us - like a wedge.

He remembered the snows of his youth. How he stood by the landing window watching the veils of amorphous whiteness sifting in silence past the amber street-lamps. He wondered about his parents, how they didn't understand his fascination and mocked him for his obsession with the weather. It was January, the month of the double-headed God, the deity that looked both ways. Was this birth or was it death? He didn't see the past as in the past, nor the future yet to come. In eternity time was nothing. The blink of the eye of a God covered more than he knew of history, was longer than from Alpha to Omega. He knew that time was timeless. Everything that happened, happened now. All was simultaneous. It was dawn by the River Chelmer, by Ulting church. The snow was crisp underfoot and the willow's slender branches were locked and leafless in the river's crystal. He could smell the frost. His living breath, cool and condensing in the still, cold air, hung like an apparition. Everything was ghosted. Trees were wreathed in mist. Gold and blue glittered in the rising sun, but as yet, death was the answer to each frozen question. In the silence he remembered the roses, the wild roses of June, real in the summer of his gilded mind. Truth was his imagination. Earth, air, fire and water; the cycles of the seasons, the cycles of our lives, the correspondences. Truth and beauty, they were fixed, eternal, every moment held all moments. But what were moments?

Moments inferred time, sequence. No, everything was cyclic, not linear. The coiled snake devouring its own tail. Curved space, infinite yet somehow bounded. He thought of the galaxies, billions of them, drifting apart on the skin of some intangible balloon, expanding into nothing, into nowhere. He knew that it had happened before, but before did not exist, no more than after. Expansion and contraction. Entropy and organisation. Heat death and the rekindling breath of God. The snowdrops caught his eye. They seemed to him to be the expression of a thought. Energy and matter, two sides of the same universal coin. Each the alter image of the other. The white heads hung in the soundless air. What were they made of? Atoms, and far, far more. The closer you look the smaller the particles. Smaller and smaller, infinitely regressing. What is a wave? What is Energy? He knew that all was thought, intelligence. 'As above, so below'. 'What you see you are'. Everything, the individuation of a thought, himself, the snowdrops, ideas in the mind of God. God's desire to experience the material world, to come to the knowledge of his own divinity. The snowdrops seemed like bells, cast in purity, ringing the changes of a bitter month. Across the frozen fields lapwings flashed like semaphore. Meanings, a code, something to decipher. Plovers, from the Latin *pluvia*, rain. Rain would be welcome now, now when the ground has a solid heart, when water

7

is brittle, and fish know a torpor that is close to non-existence.

Epiphany. Christ appears to the Gentiles. Gold, frankincense and myrrh. Wise Men and a Star. Portents and possibilities. Literal or symbolic? He didn't mind. He was a Christian, an Anglican, went to church regularly and partook of the sacraments. Sometimes he was a Gnostic, saw the snowdrops as manifest, the moon as Sophia, the sunlight's icy glitter in the dawn as nothing more or less than love's rebirth. And yet, he believed in the Wise Men, the Child and the Virgin Mother. Literally. No room in the inn. Love is like that. The pain of childbirth. The joy of new life. All is duality on earth, there is no pleasure without pain, no God without the Devil. He knew that life was a test, a conundrum, a journey. The Wise Men knew all there was to know about travel. Like the star they'd come hard miles from the east, travelled above the snowline, thirsted and hungered. They knew that revelation was a struggle, that nothing comes to those who do not labour. The snow was falling fast. Between him and the window was the tree. He started to remove the decorations. Baubles and lights, fripperies and tinsel. Outside a fox was barking. He thought of the depth and density of night, of winter's heartless grip, the darkness and the diamond weight of frost. He put a carol on the CD player. Good King Wenceslas. Hope amidst severity. Warmth in the bitter precincts of Boreas. The festival was over. Spring a distant dream and the worst cold to come. What was the difference, Saturnalia, Christmas? Topsy turvy or boy bishops? Light in the darkness is something we all need. Ancient Rome or modern London, it's all the same, feelings never alter. He thought of his faith and what the priest would think if he discovered his Pagan sympathies. The evergreen made sense to him. The holly. The thorns and berries commandeered for Christ. Blood and a token crown. He believed in the imagery but knew that it went far deeper. Father Christmas had a prelapsarian lineage. The Old Man of the greenwood. Wild and free with his bounty of ivy and mistletoe. A memory of sacred kings, of blood and sacrifice. Herod was not the first to stain his hands. Blood is our history, death our *raison d'etre*. The snow had stopped falling. He walked out into the garden and looked up at the living stars. Orion stepped out across the frosty sky. The eternal hunter with darkness as his quarry. He knew that the moon was a Goddess. Rock is the rational mind. Orbits and tides an illusion. He spoke to her gently. She was the giver of poems. Whenever he wrote he felt her presence. Her icy inspiration thawed his mind. He didn't write the weather, it wrote him. He was an expression of the snow. A manifestation of crystal, individual, and yet whole. He was ready for bed. His bones ached with the cold, his eyes were tired and heavy, and his frosted breath had turned his beard to ice. The artistry of winter etched his windows. The tracery of zero bleared the panes as he closed the curtains; shut out the moon, the reveries of starlight. Dream or reality, who's to know? Now for the little death that we call sleep. He drifted deep, deep to the frozen halls of the non-living. The Ice Queen held out her arms. Beckoned him to touch her heart's frigidity, to know the sensuality of death. But he wasn't dead. Cold, but not dead. Rime enveloped everything. Grass was thickly furred. Mist amongst the naked branches froze into spicules made of glints and glitters. Was he awake or asleep? Alive or dead? He could hear his breath rising and falling in the hoary night. Was it yesterday or tomorrow? No, it was now, always now. Now with the starlight arcing across his synapses. Now with the subtle whispers of the Gods telling the stories that were never told. Zero was absolute, but the heat death couldn't conquer. He turned in his bed like an ox being roasted on a spit and his cold subconscious flickered and drifted into warm oblivion.

The snow had melted and the wind assumed a southerly direction. By Mucking Church, by the south wall bordering the graveyard, a single daffodil had opened in the sun. Alone among the snowdrops and the aconites without a bee to pollinate its fanfare. He'd never seen a daffodil so early. Could not believe it to be meaningless. Knew that it was a portent or an omen. He must write about this new life, this message from the stars. Why was it here? Why was he here? It was Gabriel's Horn, receiver and transmitter of the Gods. A Lent Lily, so soon. Why now? Why in the midst of death this resurrection? He wandered further on, under the leafless trees, and out into the vistas of water and phragmites. The sun and breezes shattered the sacred glass. Blond reeds whispered their winter words and gnats convolved in spirals made of air. What could he say? What could he dare on such a day as this? White puffs of cloud powdered the sky's blue countenance and a deluded lark lifted the intermittence of a song. 'All's right with the world'. He thought. Boreas no longer wears his ermine. He is robed in his warm aurora, dormant and distant in some Polar dream. His mind's screen was haunted by the wings of swallows. Chiff-chaffs sang in his open ears, and time was compressed by the thoughts of swifts and nightingales. Winter was another dream, another time, or timeless. He could see his face in the water, doubled and distant like a look remembered. Who was he? Was he the wings of swallows? Migration or transmigration? A golden rudd lifted from the depths, levitated an instant in mid-air, then smashed the moment's mirror. Concentric rings radiated outwards, each gold circumference widening to infinity. This was the stars. This was the sun. This was the way the Word had its transmission. Waves that interlink as they expand and then contract in infinite pulsations. He could hear the daffodil. Not a sound exactly, not a voice, more like an intuition. An imagined bee was its vocal chords. Communication an insect. God's own mind spoken from inside a flower. 'Intimations of immortality' carried on incredulous wings. A velvet angel humming its Annunciation. He was alone like the daffodil, out of season, out of place. But his mind was a honeycomb. The bee at the centre, sweetness and procreation, pollen and seed, flowers everlasting. He walked back to the car, got in, and took out his notebook. Every detail must be entered, every nuance. His life depended on it; meaning must be wrested from the seemingly chaotic. 'Mysterious ways' indeed. God had spoken through a flower. Why him? Why now? It's that word again. Now. Snowdrops, daffodils, roses. Purity, gold and the Virgin herself. The Mystical Rose, the fragrance of the soul. He drove home in a daze. Everything was done automatically. He'd been a driver for more than forty years but now he couldn't remember where he'd been or where exactly he was going. He remembered nothing of the journey and yet arrived home safely. He put the car into the garage, went into the lounge, sat in front of the word-processor, took out his notebook and began to write.

Snow was falling again. Winter had returned. His poem was written but was somehow meaningless. Spring had been overcome. Eight inches of even snow had fallen overnight and was still falling. The garden pond was frozen solid and tits and finches fluttered and scurried for nuts and bacon-rind. The King of the North was back. Winter was ineluctable. Would not release its grip. How can hope become so hopeless? One day, twenty four hours, enough to choke the aconite with ice, enough to freeze the purpose of the sun. Is this living? Will the badger survive, the fox, the hedgehog? Will I survive, he thought? Writing is not survival, words on a page, sequences, moments recorded. It is dead as soon as it is written. Relics for future generations. Myths, memories, memento mori, curiosities only. Why would the living bother with his words? Just ink and paper. Hints of God, no more. But we never die, we're never born. The snow across the lawn was like an unwritten page. What else could he do? Books were all he had, all he knew. 'All poetry is fiction', or so he'd heard. 'But enjoy the fiction, live the fiction, and who knows you may have a revelation from nature and learn something about the supreme fiction'. Is that God's story, he thought? Is everything a story? No, stories have beginnings, middles and endings. Eternity can't be written only felt. His words began to crystallise. His inner field was in contact with the outer. He and the weather were one. A blackbird settled on the pear tree, dislodging lumps of snow. He revelled in the contrast. For him the world had always been a grey area, but now there was definition, everything was black and white, hard edged and concise. He stopped writing and went out into the garden. It was snowing so heavily that separate flakes were barely distinguishable. But it didn't seem to matter. His blood was cold and every corpuscle six-sided. His skin was white, whiter than a lily. He took off his clothes, stood naked in the middle of the lawn, and watched as the snowflakes melted on his body. This was chastity. A pure and virginal whiteness. His body was not Eros it was Agape. Lust was purely temporal. This was Love, Love of the highest order. A robin started to sing. Sad and melancholy perhaps, but to him it was 'a melancholy joy'. The robin sings all year, a bird for all seasons. Here in the cold, in the ice, naked as the day that he was born, he listened to the voice of the eternal. Spring or summer, autumn or winter, what did it matter? The song is always warm, the spheres of light commensurate with music. He started to turn blue and his flesh began to sting. It didn't last. Soon he was numb. His thoughts and the thoughts of snow became a unity. The silence and the snow-vaulted cathedrals of the trees, all conspired to increase his sense of sanctity. If this was death, then it was the death that he had longed for. The sun appeared momentarily through a rift in the clouds and a white dove feathered the air with its thawing pinions. Was this a vision or reality? Truth or a gilded dream? He didn't know. He didn't care. He turned from his tomb of ice and walked back into the house. The clock was ticking, but he didn't hear it. The month was nearing its end. But what month was it? Who decided on months anyway? Why should we turn the timeless into time? Without a thought the robin knows the answer. The snow is aware of summer's latent showers. His body was starting to sting again and he began to shiver. He looked in the mirror and saw a daffodil, a bee with angel's wings, a rose and a nightingale. Life was a strange affair. There was more to the world than appearances. A brittle tear fell from his frozen cheek, and a deep, chill sigh, bloomed on the airwaves like the flush of petals.

FEBRUARY

Lost

The woods are dead. Above - the branches etch
A cloudy sky. Below - the mould is mixed
With winter rain. Each root is like a ketch

Beneath its mast - where tattered sails are shaken
By the wind and single leaves are pennants
In the blast. A squirrel leaves its wake

Among the twigs - as like a wave it wends
Across the air - then comes to rest. We take
Our bearings deep within the glade and send

Our subtle Morse between the trees. A sketch
Is all we ask - a mental chart - a fix.
We need to save our souls beneath this fetch -

Where drowning thoughts are sifted through the brake
And aspiration - crippled by the bends.

As cold as Candlemas. Why does the Virgin need purification? She is purer than purity, whiter than frost. 'February fill the dyke be it black or be it white'. Rain or snow, Christ will be presented at the temple. He thought of the consecrated candles. The Light of the World; fire in the heart of ice. The frost was melting in the early sunlight. Crocuses were harbingers of spring. Golden gapes, begging for food, for the nourishment of heaven. He sat on a bench by the green and watched them growing. They shouldered the iron ground, shifted the soil, basked in the rays of their solar being. Eight minutes between them and their God. Ninety-three million miles, and there they were, products of hydrogen and helium; a nuclear thought. He just stared and stared. They were imprinted on his retina. Aureate petals from the stars. Visions of the cosmic dance. He stood up and moved between them. A traveller through the galaxies of gold, the firmament of being and belonging. The collared-doves were singing. Soft syllables, so redolent of heat, that he could smell the summer and the roses. Fragrance or music? The year's first blackbird scented the air with sound. What he heard he could see, what he saw he heard. He walked beneath the elms, the diseased elms, the dead elms. But he could not believe in death. Not now with the crocuses and the blackbird's sweet vitality. The blueness was intense. Sapphire, cerulean, azure. He was infused with blueness. As buoyant as the blackbird's song. Lifted to the lyric heights of wonder; high and ecstatic in the sky's circumference. He took a few cautious steps. The ground had left him. Gravity was non-existent. Was this the astral plane? Insouciance was all. Carefree and careless with the heart enlightened. Swallows were in his brain. Intuitive shapes, fletched with the feathers of the sun, silent yet substantial. Time had been breached again. The sun was a yellow rose. Swifts in his mind's eye, were bees in the perfume of the warming air. He floated back to earth. Light, a translucent music. Birdsong, a reference point for heat. The gates were open, perception viable. Anything was possible. Summer was in the bud, and in his thoughts. Frost was the Devil's geometry; the sorcery of crystal. The meridian was warm. The first of the celandine opened their moistened eyes. A brimstone butterfly, teetered on the edges of existence, trembled, then was gone. There was no need to speak, the dream was audible. Sound was the words of grass, and the early daisies, muted yet meaningful. 'If winter comes'. He closed his eyes. Felt the sun on his brow. This was a God indeed. Thrones and Dominions, Powers and Principalities. Again he heard the lark; a seraph on the wings of song, a full stop in the infinite blueness, an end to the paragraphs of winter. He opened his eyes. The light was dazzling, the essence of Heraclitus, ignis fatuus, St Elmo's fire. He was burning with passion, aflame with desire. He stretched out his arms in the shape of a crucifix, hung on the air for an agonising instant, then died to the death of flesh. His spirit suckled at his mother's breast. His father stepped out of singularity and shone in the darkness, like a supernova. The birth of the universe and a death. Alpha to Omega, beginnings and endings, endings and beginnings. Genesis and Revelations, all in the moment's mind, turning forever through the wheels of starlight.

A February dusk. Venus in the west, a crescent moon over the sea, and sentiments of frost in light's subconscious. This night would chill his spirit. The temperature would drop, fathom to zero and the densities below. Ice would form its crystals on the tide-line, and the saltings creak in winter's harsh debacle. He could hear the curlew from his window. Soulful and solitary, like the death of hope. The widgeon whistled, faint from the distant mud-banks, almost a silence, almost a sound. The moon-glade rippled in the flood and a skein of ghostly geese crossed the illumined palm with frozen silver. He stood on his doorstep. Looked down towards the sea, the stars, and the wandering planets. He had fished these very waters, times beyond remembrance. Summer days, out by the Maplin Sands, riding the swatchways in the search of bass. Such heat now seemed incongruous. The glittering scales of the fish, fired in sunlight, like a thousand mirrors. He had fished in the drowning darkness, deep in the freezing depths of December, the mouths of cod surfacing like silent screams, hooked by the moonlight and a frosted gaff. But now it seemed lifeless. The cold was too intense, the ice too heavy. He made his way down to the shore. The breakers whispered with crystals in their throats. Life was a pair of swans, two shadows and the sound of wings, earthing the moment to the mythic ether. He threw a pebble out into the darkness. Water was smithereens, shards of moonlight, smashed and refracted into brittle silver. The water calmed. Silence happened. This was the void he feared. Nothing, no space, no time, no substance, nothing. What is nothing? Perhaps it's the mind of God. The dazzling darkness. The thoughtless all-knowing. Everything comes from nothing. How could that be, he thought, how could nothing have potential, be the root of all that's raised and manifested? He stopped thinking. An oystercatcher bleeped, a spark in the core of ice, something living, something intelligible. The saltings were sheeted with ice, and ice-floes lifted and fell with the swell of the tide. Everything seemed to shimmer. A million points of coruscating silver, the shining ones, the deities of zero. Again he could smell the frost. How to explain the fragrance, the subtlety, the perfume never captured by his pen, the scent that haunted all unwritten pages? Words or the want of them.

His mind was frozen. The stars were his lexicon, but he didn't understand them, could not decipher light at such a distance. Was he really alone? Did the horizons lead to nowhere? Was The Bear a figment, Orion a lost and silent constellation? He made his way home. Splinters of frost fell and glistened in the glow of the street-lamps. Cats were caterwauling. A dustbin lid clattered, and a foraging fox vanished as quickly as the sound subsided. He opened the door, turned on the light, and sat in his favourite chair. He thumbed a pinch of tobacco into his pipe, lit up, and took a relaxing draw. The cold had entered his room, had entered his imagination. Soon he would have to sleep, never to wake perhaps, never to know the languages of frigidity. He fluffed up his pillows, lay back, and looked at the shadows on the ceiling. He thought that he saw a rose. A black rose. He turned off the light and closed his eyes. Sleep came swiftly. His ghosted breath hung in the silence on the edge of substance, and then deformed, dispersed, and disappeared.

The scudding clouds followed the prevailing winds. The vaporous air was rinsed and wrung, and the slanting rain pattered against his window. It was mild for the time of year. The buds on the elder trees stretched in their green seams. The celandine closed their eyes in the absence of the sun, and a storm-cock rocked to its rhythms in the swaying branches. 'Fill the dyke' indeed. All was torrential. Time for the river and the winter spates. He got into his car and headed north. The windscreen-wipers were a metronome, keeping time with the downpour, and restricted vision. Spray was everywhere. He could see, and he couldn't see. Trees were overarching and diffuse, fields a blur, and horizons non-existent. He arrived at Hoe Mills. The river had burst its banks. Meadows were inundated, the road a raging torrent, and the lock-gates useless under the weight of the breaking waters. He loved a flood. He loved extremes in general. Something out of the ordinary. Something to make you see; to make you feel. A motley group of domestic geese and ducks cropped at the edges of the swollen river. In summer they would glide beneath the willows and the alders, upend themselves and dabble for provisions. Would it ever be as calm again? Would the swans still swim serenely with their signets? Would the sunlight glitter in the shallows? He couldn't think of lily-pads or loosestrife. This viscous water was his blood. The savagery and drench of this sou'wester was coursing through his arteries and lungs, and he was happy to drown, content to float and waver with the weeds. The skies opened. The rain came down in swathes. Bubbles formed and burst in unnumbered congregations. Bubbles like thoughts. Sacrificial and sacred. Washed in the blood of winter, borne by the bread of the sunken grain. A transubstantiation. Air into isinglass. Rain into reasons and untold reflections. He was dripping from head to foot. His hair tangled and tousled and matted. Water streamed down his face. His sopping clothes were treble their normal weight. Water oozed between his toes and out through the seams of his shoes. He didn't care. He was like the winter pike, his range had been extended; he was free of the confines of the shoals and margins. Now he could roam. Weave between the stranded trees and bushes. Swim through the grasses of another world. Feed on the sediments that fed the soul. He was a river God. Rudd were the rubies on his fingers. Perch his gleaming jade. Bream his soliloquies of silver. Nothing would ever be the same; he was away from the land, the material. Here it was water, deep and dark and spiritual. He could drown in his own subconscious; sink into the archetypes, dream in the half-light with the shoals of roach. Fish held the answer, he knew they did. Were the rudd not golden, the dace not silver? This was the medium for mediums. Contact could be made. Beneath the surface skin, the glittering shallows. He was ninety per/cent water. Depth was his element. Water his very being. He imagined he was growing gills. He could breathe in the soundless halls. He was chilling as he sank, deeper and deeper through the thermocline. His blood and the water and the mud had all combined. He was in a state of torpor. He lay among the silts and the cabbage-weed. A freshwater mussel opened before his unbelieving eyes, and a perfect pearl, shimmered with iridescence, like a star in winter.

Black or white, white or black? A black rose, a white rose? The snows came on again. Would winter ever end, did it ever begin? Once more the garden was sunk in the weight of whiteness. This time the wind had been behind it. Enormous drifts lapped across the hedgerows and the fences, and hung in their fluted shapes, like the gills of sub-arctic fungi. The blown snow emptied the nearby fields, and the smoking ounces built to a burden in the lee of any structure. Form and formlessness. Amorphous or defined. He'd heard it called a white-out, but it was intermittent. At times like an icy fog, blurring the edges of a hidden meaning. And then a lull. Calm and definition. Trees like iron cages, holding the hunch of dishevelled birds. Telegraph-poles and wires, etched against pewter skies, loping and looping into crystal distances. Sound, like a banshee; and then no sound at all. The window was between him and a blackbird. More than a window perhaps. More like the laws of evolution, or creation, who knows? Would the blackbird survive? Would its song thaw the air-waves on the edge of blossom? What is survival anyway? How many lives had he had? How many creatures had he been? Would he ever become an angel; a God? The wind had dropped. A thin light haloed the diffuse sun. He walked into the garden. Birds scattered in his wake, seraphim and cherubim, cloaked in the diaphanous, gossamer and starlight, shimmers and translucence. These were the wings of angels. Whiteness's and gilded feathers. Pinions of ice splayed into the essences of light, were soft in the muted air. He decided to build a snowman. It would take him back, or forward, he wasn't sure. The snow was cold in his hands and that which thawed soon froze to an icy sheen. The snowman's body had taken on the gloss of a frosted glass. He could see his image in the snowman's image. How strange to remember and forget. He was there, he was five years old. He was crying with the cold, his fingers were stinging and his toes were nearly numb. But he didn't want to go indoors, he had to finish building the snowman, everything depended on it. It was the same now; it would always be the same. He finished the snowman. Hat and scarf, coal for buttons, a carrot for a nose. He turned away to go but something caught the corner of his eye. The snowman had moved. He was sure. He hadn't imagined it. Was it only in story-books? Never in the real world, whatever the real world is? If he believed it would be true. And true it was. The snowman held out his hands and the poet gripped them tight. They danced. A dance of never-ending circles. Snow was in their eyes, but they didn't care. Faster and faster they whirled. They were vortices, spirals, the double-helix itself. They spun through the eye of a galaxy, hovered by a black-hole, danced with the field and quadrilled with the darkest matter. They were the event horizon. They were the boundary. They spun and they spun and they spun and the entire universe spun with them. They didn't need to breathe, they didn't melt; they didn't freeze too much. This was the cosmic dance. The more they spun the lighter they were. Particles shed in all directions. They were not matter, they were not waves, they were energy; pure energy. Boreas flew by on the back of Pegasus, laughing and laughing, his aurora flowing out behind him. Buddha danced with Christ. Mohammed held Jehovah by the beard and they swirled into starlight like the Whirling Dervishes. The dance slowed, vibrations were heavier. Time reasserted itself. The snowman stood at the edge of dusk, perfectly still, perfectly frozen. The poet was exhausted. He walked back into the house. Shot a backward glance at his former self; his youth in aspic. He was close to tears. Winter would soon be gone. Death or birth? He didn't know. Another life was ahead of him. Adolescence a possibility, death another. Old March of Many Weathers called his name, and off he strode through bumble-bees and flowers.

MARCH

Star Gazer

Though sedentary - I travel: this garden
Links its language to the stars - and I must
Think with gravity - and purpose. We are

It seems from light years - and in part - the substance
And submission of the sun. The cosmos
And its procreative heart still dance the dance -

Particulate - and pure - that counts the cost
Of energy and mass: delimits chance.
I cannot think - not here - with thoughts of loss -

When spiders weave the sunlight - as they pass -
And I perceive the permanence of dust.
This flower - is like looking - in a glass:

I see Orion's stride - his cosmic stance -
And think - no more - of winter: and its frost.

What can be said of March? A young man's fancy, an old man's dream. The rooks are back in the elms. A parliament of love. A gathering of inceptive spirits. It was March when he met his love. So many years ago, or was it? It seems he has always been in love, like the daffodils and the bees, the frogs croaking in the garden pond. How blond she is, how blue her eyes. Skin like the whitest lilies, the remembered snow. He knew her before she was born. He will know her after she dies. This is the month of the first arrivals. The migrants from the south, the harbingers of song. Is the March hare mad? He didn't think so. It was ecstatic, crazed with the thought of love. The blossom was on the plum. The celandine were trading gold and pollen. He had to capture this. Preserve the moment, like an insect held in amber. But words wouldn't speak the blossom, imprint the celandine. A blackbird started to sing. Golden notes from a golden bill, something to remember and forget. Why was time against him? Why would the words not come? She was so beautiful and he was so much in love. Was he in love with her, or with love itself? He wasn't sure. He wasn't sure about anything. The frogs were croaking in the pond and he wasn't sure. The bees were in the daffodils and he wasn't sure. The celandine were sunlight in the shadows and he wasn't sure. Like that daffodil in January, alone and out of place. He was that flower. In love and yet somehow on his

28

own, somehow lonely. He walked towards the pond, stealthily. A dozen male frogs clung to a single female. This didn't seem like love, more like a primal force, more like lust. He clapped his hands and the frogs disengaged, submerged in an instant. All he could see were their eyes, staring in his direction, fearful and alert. Did they know who he was, who they were? Had God endowed them with vision as well as sight? Was this just instinct, a blind adherence to a law, a law that they weren't privy to? He could see his face in the depths, vague; nebulous, distant. Who was he? 'As above so below', 'what you see you are'. He saw the reflection of the moon. A petal fallen from the plum. Was it rock or a Goddess? He was drowning. A goldfish rippled through his eyes, swam into the moon. A newt surfaced, gazed vacantly, wriggled its sinuous body; then disappeared. He would have to write this down, this was important, meaningful. But what did it mean? He sensed something, something near, something imminent. He awoke from his reveries, turned around and looked back towards the house. There she was, framed in the doorway. An image of the moon, sunlight in her golden hair, her eyes the firmament. This was love, not desire for the flesh, but a longing for the spirit. She smiled. Everything altered. This was not chance, not adaptation, not the survival of the fittest. He looked around him. Everything was sharp, clear, delineated. Design was gilded. A rose bloomed in the vacuum and scented the timeless moment. He picked it with his mind and offered it to his beloved. She was the Virgin, the Mystical Rose. Her eyes were petals. Her hands were thorns. He followed the rose deep into her consciousness. He was scratched and bleeding but he didn't care. Somewhere in the depth of her mind, in the continuum of her thoughts, he felt at peace. He was no longer himself and she had relinquished her personhood. The fragrance was starlight. The darkness, dazzling. Thoughts were replaced by feelings, by the senses. Words were unnecessary. He was the poem, the petals, the perfume. The frogs began to croak again. His lips were touching hers. Love was a pure vibration.

March winds. The invisible made visible. He remembered his adolescence. The marshes and the great elms. The clouds, like lions, prowling from west to east, and the bleat of the first spring flowers as they raced through the shadows in the rippling pastures. Fleets and dykes were stirred by the slant of the wind. Shimmering sliver; gold in the sudden sunlight. Then his thoughts were simple. Complexity didn't occur to him. All was sun and cloud and water. Nothing but light and amorphous substance. The high elms snapped wood against the wind. Rooks were black diagonals into air. Sound was raucous. He remembered a pair of swans, infinite swans, eternal swans, mythic swans. Their wings were raised to catch the blast and they sailed over silver like a double hallmark. Light was cut like diamonds, hard edged, crystalline. Had the swans been formed by snowflakes? Were their feathers cast in frost? Was their disposition icy? Those days were still with him. He was there in his imagination. It was reality, not nostalgia. He decided to go back, to retrace his adolescent footsteps. He drove down the lane towards the marshes. The once overarching elms had succumbed to Dutch elm disease and were now no more than bushes. But that was the dream, the illusion. In his mind time did not exist. The elms were the same height, the rooks the same rooks. St Margaret's Church, unaltered since his childhood. Norman stone, ragstone, timeless geological stone. Their were tribes on the edges of ideas. A vast moraine, glacial melt-water, spears and woolly mammoths. A curlew called from a distant creek. Solitary. Mournful. Cattle browsed on the first spring grasses. A skylark climbed the rungs of Jacob's ladder, became a sunspot. He could hear the wind through the reeds. See the substance of the wind. See movement. He remembered the rudd of his youth. The golden moments set with rubies, spinning in mid-air. He could remember letting them go. Animate jewels dissolving in silver. The wind was taking his breath away. The force of invisibility, holding him back; ruffling his hair. Was this the breath of God? Was this the weather's word, the unwritten meaning? He didn't know, but it didn't matter. He was here, where he'd always been. The bleat of the flowers, the prowling clouds. He'd written it more than once, but the words and the experience were different. Were the difference between naming and being, between isolation and belonging. He could smell the distant sea. Gulls curved and cried in the wind, like lost souls. He walked through the cattle; they stopped chewing the cud, and eyed him suspiciously. They were clouds themselves. Black and white clouds moving slowly through the pasture, nebulous, amorphous, shifting shapes. A kestrel hovered and a bank vole foraged unawares. Death is as sudden as that he thought. It happens while you're looking the other way, takes you by surprise. Death or birth he didn't know. Forever or once, spiritual or temporal? He made his way back to the car. His clothes were flapping in the wind. His breath was uneven. Air, all there was between him and eternity, or oblivion. The biosphere, a few thousand feet to live in, to know, to believe in or not depending on nature, culture, who knows? He started the engine and the sun's resources remembered their origins. Combustion, all is combustion. Heraclitus was right. The sun and the wind flaring in the creeks. The swans on fire. The rooks still aureate in remembered tree-tops.

The equinox was upon him. Equal day and equal night. A pagan festival. The Green Man was stirring. The carvings in the church came to life. He wandered down the aisle and knelt in front of the altar. Christ crucified and the Green Man, death and resurrection. Darkness and light, dimensions of the mind, duality. Vases were full of flowers; cuckoo-flowers, ground-ivy, celandine and sweet violets. He could smell the violets; they smelt of Lent, had the colour of Lent. Where were the Lent-lilies, the daffodils? Were they saving them for Easter Sunday? The sacrament was reserved. A red light swung in the moted air. Flame and glass. Body and blood. Osiris or Christ? Sacrificed and resurrected. Reborn in the spirit. Murder or symbolism? Mass or energy? The Green Man was stirring, leaves were respondent, roses in the bud. He thought of the offices, matins to vespers; light between the darkness. Equal day and equal night. Lucifer and Christ. He began to pray. Father save me from myself, give me the thoughtless thought, banish the darkness; fill me with the sun, the stars, the moon. He was the Green Man, the gargoyles, the crucifix. He went to the Virgin chapel. The statue of Our Lady wasn't stone. A tear fell from her eye and blossomed on her cheek. The Mystical Rose. Mother, he said, suckle me. Fill me with the Milky Way, let me live on your love's lactation. Flesh and bone dissolved, he was a body of light, immaterial. He was in the realm of angels:

cherubim and seraphim, powers and principalities. God and Christ were on the throne and the Holy Ghost bathed them in golden light, diffuse and diaphanous. Ivy twined about them. Their haloes were garlanded with flowers. Trees produced silver fruits, like the moon, none of them forbidden. Adam and Eve were one, neither male nor female, neither flesh nor blood. Sin was impossible. Everyone, everything, partook of the Virgin. Chastity, purity, eternal love. All was born of the spirit, even the serpent's scales were shimmering and translucent. There were no shadows; they were a thing of the earth, an illusion. Darkness and light had been resolved. All was silver and gold, sunlight and stars. This is the mystery of faith. Let us Pray. Peace be with you. Thought was returning, relationships were being named. He was stealing the essence of things. What he thought they were he described, and in describing they became something else, something alien. His world was populated, duality had returned and he was isolate and alone. He left the church and walked out into the gathering dusk. The air was still and the first stars iridesced. Tonight would be a night of frost. The moon would be a black rose, a dead rose, and the shooting stars would tear his flesh apart. He was not Osiris. He was not Christ. His flesh was mortal and his blood began to freeze.

March was coming to an end. Although almost imperceptible, the days were gaining in strength. A chiff-chaff sang in the copse by the river. Soon he would hear the willow warbler, each falling cadence as sweet as the sun on water. Was this birth or death? The rose was in the bud, but the night still held the sentiment of frost. It didn't matter; the sun was shining, the song thrush singing, and the breeze all but a whisper in the rushes. What was it whispering? What were the mute iambics trying to say? The river was all reflections. Moorhens ticked like clockwork from one bank to the other. A water-vole made vees in velvet. Coots bickered. The river was an icon. He scried the glass and meditated. There were swallows in his mind. They skimmed across his winter thoughts, their blue ecstatic backs tempered by the summer yet to come. Where were the golden lilies, the damsel-flies? They were where they'd always been, always and everywhere. He was four seasons all rolled up in one. Leaves on the river's surface were a red and gold mosaic. The sun through mist, a monstrance. Glittering ice; love's fire. A robin started to sing, autumn in spring, sadness and joy together. Soon it would be the cuckoo and cuckoo spit. The yaffle would be laughing again, splitting his sides, and gilding the fields of rape. A perch passed beneath his gaze. Green with vertical stripes. Red finned in the gloom. Melting into the mirror. Coots crashed amongst the rushes, iconoclasts, shatterers of image and reflection. A barge, laden with wood, cut a swathe through the rippling silver, and torn reeds and rushes bobbed up and down in its wake. All was jetsam he thought. Debris and detritus. Incidents and accidents. Pieces only; parts of the puzzle. On the other side of the river, in the water-meadows, a pair of March hares raced and revelled in the sun, boxed in ever-decreasing circles. Were they mad? He didn't think so. Love was the only answer. Kingcups assayed their own gold and a peewit wove and whistled on the air. How could they be the same? A flower and a song. All he could see was difference; individuality. This was the time for Zephyr and Flora, for Boreas and Anemone. Winter and spring together, two seasons, two hearts, one warm, one cold. The anemones are not frigid, they open for Boreas, wind-flowers in the frost, harbingers and hoary like this month. West wind and flowers, sunlight on the river, snow at midnight. Old March Many Weathers. What could he do? He too blew hot and cold. He looked back into the river and a silver rose bloomed before his very eyes. A sunken rose. A scentless rose. A rose in isinglass. Was the river liquid or solid, water or glass or ice? He didn't know. The chiff-chaff filled the air with repetitions. This had happened before, will happen again, has always happened. A brimstone butterfly powdered the air with yellow wings. Water and light scintillated. A water-vole surfaced, then submerged. There were swallows in his mind, always swallows, skimming his winter thoughts, bringing the breath of summer in their wake. Roses and nightingales, warblers and cuckoos. He could hear the breeze through the rushes. What was it trying to say? What was the language in its susurrations? The world was Babel and birdsong. He spread his arms as if to fly. Icarus or an angel? He didn't know. He wanted to fly into the sun, to integrate, to merge his nuclear being. His wings, his imagination. Would they melt? Would he survive? He was a being of the sun, the sun was his God, and he himself was the sun. There was after all no difference; the fire and the flame are one. The immolation wasn't painful, he didn't burn. He sank through the sunspots, was helium then hydrogen. Whose mind was this? Whose atoms of thought? Whose particles of infinite ideas, rarefied as waves and then pure energy? There were not many weathers only one. The celandine was the sun; the sun was the celandine. Phoebus was full of bees and nectar. His mind's proboscis sipped at the golden centre, and light was sweet, unsullied, and on fire.

APRIL

Black-Bird

I have heard the blackbird singing - listened
In April by the dawning sun to notes
That diminish any chance of frost. Have wished

By the blossom on the morning pear that white
Was the answer to my darkest thoughts.
How - when the leafage could repay my sight

Can the vision alter to the sum of naught
And dim the dimensions of emergent light?
Again it's the blackbird with its song unsought

Drying the dewdrops and the early mist -
Leaving me speechless in a world of ghosts.
Here on the edges that could offer bliss

I wait for the darkness of another night -
Crave for the silence - and the stars that slaughter.

This is the showery month. Glacial clouds bubbling into blue. Skylarks climbing on the wings of song. The rain had passed and he walked out into the glittering garden. A rainbow arched from horizon to horizon. You can see a rainbow, he thought, but you can't touch it. Spectral, spectrum, spectre. Light reflected and refracted at 42 degrees from the sun. White light split by the rain's prismatic droplets. He was a lover of illusions, of things not being what they appear to be. Follow the rainbow all you like, but you'll never find the end, the crock of gold. The air was diamonded. Drops of rain hung from the tips of twigs. Inside each one, deep in translucent silver, the world was inverted. He didn't understand optics, but was fascinated nevertheless. Why was the garden upside-down? Why was he upright? Why was the earth round? A cabbage-white butterfly convolved in the steaming sunlight. Why didn't it fly straight? Why the curvature, the spirals? Another cabbage-white joined in, and the pair were like snowflakes describing a double helix. All life was spirals, vortices. He looked into the raindrops and saw the galaxies reflected. Saw the curve of a comet in the blackbird's golden flight. Saw the moon in the common daisies, a shooting star quick-silvered in each bead of light. The sun drifted into the soaring cumuli and shadows dowsed the glitter and the glare. It started to rain. The blackbird's April song trembled in the lilac and laburnum. Purple smoke, golden rain, spectral music. He stood with his arms outstretched. The raindrops pattered into his palms. Transparent stigmata, nails made of air and invisible vapours. Was he deluded? No. He was crucified by the weather. He was the Christ, in amongst the Lent-lilies. A thrush's double song rose from the tomb of winter. The sun reappeared and the spectrum was manifest. There were two rainbows, one sharp and one faint. The colours were reversed, violet and red, red and violet. What was real, what was illusive? He didn't know. The weeping-cherry wept pink rain. Tulips were red tears, tears of the Gods. Daffodils were blood, yellow blood, gushing in his mind's eye, racing through the arteries of thought. Where were the bees, the velvet angels? Was this birth or death? Paradise or purgatory? He didn't know, he wasn't sure. The collared-doves were drenched, hunched up and dishevelled. Mist rose from their warming feathers. Gold-leaf shimmered with their soft syllabics. The butterflies were back, spiralling into blue, breaking the code of sunlight. He lowered his arms and walked towards the plum tree. The blossom was butterflies. White butterflies, falling and curving through the glittering air. Confetti for the marriage of the seasons. Snowflakes for memory. A chaffinch rattled its song. Sparks of sound. Fire in the branches. A greenfinch wheezed. A summer sound in spring. A union. The Muse was with him. The voice in the daffodils. The whisper in the leaves. Inspiration. Would he remember when he was at his desk? Would the words blossom, the lyric coalesce? He wasn't sure, how could he know? A skylark hovered in the blue light. A dark rose. A scented song. Black petals on a golden stem. Sunlight and thorns. A poem that's lost its language. He went back indoors. The clock was ticking, but time stood still. He went into the kitchen and poured himself a glass of water. As he drank, droplets dribbled down his chin. The light through the kitchen window split through each tiny prism. Spectrum, spectra, spectres.

A cuckoo flew across the fields of rape. His song was doubled and the rape was doubled in the river. 'Oh to be in England!' The wise thrush was duplicated music. The cuckoo's bell rang and echoed and resounded. Fish were concentricity, waves, a velvet radiation. Could the world hold so much gold? Would the sunlight sizzle and dissolve? Would darkness be the answer to reflections? He thought he heard a nightingale. A song that issued from the greening thorn; the Queen-Anne's-lace. He could smell the parsley, the earth, the wild garlic. An orange-tip fluttered along the hedgerow. A flake of sunlight. Snow and fire in equal measure. Pollen was everywhere, in the air, on his lips, on his tongue. He could taste it, smell it; feel its golden touch. The future was in the pollen, and the past. Fruits and seeds, seeds and

41

fruits. The apple unbitten. Flesh without sin. Love in a haunted garden. An adder coiled in the sun, grateful for the early warmth. Poison without venom. Prelapsarian beauty. The year's first warblers twittered in the reeds. He listened to each vibration, air made resonant. Sound was an illusion, a miracle of air. What could he do? Was there no vacuum? Was silence impossible? He could hear the sun, the golden audibility. Waves, all waves. His cells were resonating, reaching out into the cosmos. He couldn't see the stars but he could hear them. Sirius a repeated note. A double bell, a vibrating echo. Cuckoo! cuckoo! He worried about his love, his star child. Was she with someone else? Was there anyone else? Who was she? Who was he? He didn't know, he wasn't sure. Cuckoo! cuckoo! He wandered into the churchyard. Dandelions were gold doubloons, bounty from the Gods. The church walls were worn and weathered. Headstones and iron crosses tilted at different angles. Lichen and moss softened and suffused. Time and timelessness, here by the river, here in the graveyard. Eliza Gossett, accidentally killed by fire. Poor Eliza, a star child killed by fire. Don't worry Eliza, you can't be killed by fire. You are fire, everything is fire; everything is sunlight. Did you know me before Eliza? Will you know me again? Have you always known me? A green woodpecker hammered at the shingles on the spire. The star of Bethlehem blossomed in his mind. A barge full of day-trippers passed by slowly. People waved, he waved back. He didn't know them, they didn't know him - or did they? He picked a star of Bethlehem, the green sepals, the white petals, perfection. Cuckoo! cuckoo! He thought he heard a nightingale. The green woodpecker hammered again; then flew off in a gale of laughter. Everything was still, the water motionless, the leaves listless and silent. This was the first real warmth, a hint of things to come, dove-song and demoiselles. The first swallow dipped to its own reflection, doubled its image. 'One swallow doesn't make a summer'. But it does, it does. Summer's in the mind. In winter, in autumn, in spring. Summer's a way of seeing, a way of feeling. If you think of summer it evaporates, evanesces. He knew that the senses held it, not the thoughts. Christ was on the face of the river, golden where the breeze pawed at the rippling surface. Mohammed was in the rushes, he could hear him whispering. The river was Nirvana, a koan with a resolution. A maze into the infinite depths, the dazzling subconscious. He held out his arms and turned his palms towards the sky. A cuckoo and a nightingale settled on each hand. Day and night, sunlight and darkness, winter and spring. Cuckoo! cuckoo! He closed his eyes. Felt the sun hammering on his forehead. A skylark lifted its song into the boundless possibilities of sky, and the fields of golden rape gathered their ingots into wafts of fragrance and melted, slowly, around his holy feet.

It was Lent at All Saints. Purple drapes covered the statues and the crucifixes. There were no flowers. The church was dark, and dank, and musky. He was on his own. The vaulted roof was starless. Sunlight and shadows moved slowly through the stations of the cross. He was on his knees in the centre of the centre aisle. This was the omphalos at Delphi, the intersection of the four winds, the four elements. He fingered his rosary. Prayers susurrated from his lips. 'Holy Mary Mother of God, pray for us sinners now, and at the hour of our death'. Was this life or oblivion? A red rose budded and bloomed above him. Hung in mid-air. Was this the blood of the Virgin or the blood of Golgotha? He wasn't sure. He recited the angelus under his breath. He recited the Agnus Dei, the Gloria, the Kyrie eleison. The purple drapes were transfigured. Suffused with light and fire. He floated in the empty space. The coals of hell glimmered below him. Cerberus snapped at his heels. Three slavering heads; a trinity of canines and incisors. The sunlight slanted through the stained-glass, and the Father, the Son, and the Holy Ghost, were envisaged in the transubstantive air. 'Holy Mary Mother of God, pray for us sinners now, and at the hour of our death'. He could see right through his hands, he was transparent; he was a body of light. In the kaleidoscopic glass birds were depicted. A blackbird and a thrush clung to their sprays of blossom. They began to sing. Was this the heavenly choir? A chorus of angels? The sounds soothed his mind. He became tired. Drifted from consciousness. He awoke in the Virgin chapel. It was the time of vigil. White flowers and golden palm glittered in the flickering candle-light. Time was somewhere else, sound had been extinguished. 'Our Father who art in heaven, hallowed be thy name'. He repeated the words a thousand times, believed in the seemingly impossible. The passion was at the point of culmination. The cross, symbolic or otherwise, waited the nails and the mortal flesh. The Via Dolorosa beckoned. He stood up and walked towards the covered crucifix. He could see through the purple drapes. Could see the agony; could feel the agony. They threw dice for his belongings, poured vinegar on his wounds. Why have thou forsaken me! Why? He didn't know, he wasn't sure. Everything went dark. The pain was so intense he couldn't bear it, he passed out; he may have even died. It was Easter Morning. Daffodils garlanded the aisles. Sunlight and stained glass threw a spectral image onto the chancel floor. The priest was in white and gold. He could hear the doves cooing outside in the trees. His mind was a raised stone. The time for pietas was over. A golden rose bloomed by the hanging crucifix. Christ is dead - Christ has risen - Christ will come again.

It was St George's Day and Shakespeare's birthday. His thoughts were on England. Noblese oblige, the enclosure acts, serfs and masters, the bourgeoisie and the proletariat. The problems seemed beyond all resolution. The one and the many, a pyramid of wealth and power and status. How could a pyramid be turned on its head? Think of the instability, the lack of balance. He thought that life should be linear, that disparities should be narrowed, the consensus widened. History didn't agree. War was our lineage, violence our heritage. Perhaps the hunter gatherers had it all, were healthier than the farmers; had more time for love and culture. He didn't understand the dialectic, the interminable revisions. He could understand the fascist, the lust for power, the tyrannical mindset. But why should the collective fall apart? Why should the comrade kill his brother? 'Oh to be in England'. England and ' The wise thrush singing his song twice over'. Like the skylark, he could only rise above it, transcend the secular. Was this escapism? An avoidance of reality? Shakespeare played to the monarchs, Browning to an educated audience. He must write for himself, for God. But he was God, everything was God, there was no division. Division was illusory. Lilacs and apple-blossom. The cuckoo's double note. Constable's paintings, Crome and Cotman. The white cloud of Samuel Palmer, building into the blue, glacial, resplendent. Vaughan-Williams and Meredith, living yet in the skylark's pastoral song. Black satanic mills. Jerusalem. Slums and slag-heaps. 'A war to end all wars'. Millions dead, millions injured, Millions tormented by dark visions. Another war to end all wars. Millions dead. The Holocaust. Treblinka and Auschwitz. Stalin's Terror. Torquemada. The Crusades. 'Oh to be in England'. He walked along the byways of his youth. Jack-by-the-hedge plucked orange-tips out of nowhere. Snow and fire, ice and the flaking sun. Then he didn't think, didn't want to think, didn't need to think. He walked with the crystal tigers. Lived in the heart of flowers. Was anima and animus, archetype and essence of the sun. Now it was different. He had named his relationships. Shattered his nerves. Been broken by the irresolvable. Why is God testing him? Testing everyone? Where now the crystal tigers, the natural instincts, the primal forces, the intuitions? He must transcend it, transcend it all, his life depended on it. We learn compassion through pain, love through lovelessness. He was thinking of England, an England he loved, and hated. All was divisive; all a dilemma. He opened his window and looked out into the garden. The lilac and laburnum shimmered in the sunlight. Daffodils gathered the bees; their brown and velvet angels. Tulips were the lips of God. Lips of blood. Lips of Love. Lips of life. A blackbird started to sing. He and the song were one. He floated to the middle distance. The sun in cirrus hung like a holy wafer. The skylark's song was blithe and spiritual. He was drowning in the blue; the milky haze. Peterloo or paradise. He didn't' know, he wasn't sure. Was this death or birth? He was surrounded by swallows. Swallows and roses. 'My love is like a red, red, rose'. He had crossed a border in the mind. England was not just England. It was the place of all places. The place of imagination. The habitation of the soul, of music, of painting, and of love. He closed his eyes and the flag of St George floated in front of him. It spread out in all directions. Encompassed the earth and slowly faded. 'To be or not to be'. Was this birth or was this death? The earth began to dissolve. Starlight and sunlight were one. The hosts of heaven were not hosts. Light was all there was; light and a deep, deep, peace.

MAY

Gods

Remember - said the sun: I am the one
That warms your frozen mind - your God - your sole
Provider of the light - save for the moon -

The comets and the stars. I - am not endless:
I have duration - subservience
To time: mine is a golden blessing

For the flowers - a brilliance - an essence
Made divine. There are other Gods - oh yes -
The invisible ones - those without tense

Whose thoughts indwell - the starling and the stone.
They are the recognition of the whole
Where I - am but the builder - of your bones.

I am a God - provisional - no less -
Like you - I wait the future: my transcendence.

He walked beside the may-flowering thorns. The sky was azure and gold, the landscape green and white. May Queen or Virgin? He didn't know. The blossom was enough of purity; the scent sweet, with a hint of corruption. He nuzzled his head deep into the blooms. He could not get enough of them. This was his tree, the unlucky tree. Was this birth or death? The fragrance of a new-born child, or the smell of putrefaction. Both smells in the same flower. Life and death. Love and the loss of vision. The cuckoo's double note drifted across the hay-sweet meadows. A swallow drew an arc in the boundless blue and a skylark lifted song into the sun. He lay down in the hay, the sweet hay, and the smell of wild flowers. A cloud or two, as white as the hawthorn blossom, fathomed the sky's blue ocean, and the skylark's high cadenza rippled like water in a mountain stream. It was Beltane. Fire and the Goddess, sunlight and the flowering may. The cuckoo's double note, the skylark's song reflected in the glittering dew-ponds. The unlucky tree. Everything had its double. Was it life or death? Love was only known because of hate. Calm because of storm. Truth, a counter to the eye's deception. He closed his eyes and drifted with the fragrance and the song. The sun was reflected in a thousand ritual fires. The May Queen danced and the Sacred King scattered the seeds of life. Giggling girls and boys held on to their coloured ribbons and circled the towering oak. A yaffle laughed and a crystal tiger prowled through the sun and shadows. Whiteness was all there was, a white rose, a vision of beauty and of peace. My Love, my Eternal Lady, he said, you magnify the Lord. The rose began to smile and tears of joy, like May-Dew itself, trickled down every petal, glinted in the golden light. He could hear her whispered voice; the chastity, the charity. 'And the greatest of these is charity'. Love. Agape not Eros. This was the flowering may, the cuckoo's double note, and the skylark's high cadenza. He stood up and began to walk towards the woods, the high woods, the green woods. Red and white campion peered from the shadows like the eyes of elves. The slanted light filtered through the trees and the stitchwort stars, clustered and constellated, in their greensward heaven. Bluebells were a nether sky and he walked like a cloud amongst them. They had a faint smell, a sweetness, a serenity. Again he lay down. Two skies, two of everything. The cuckoo's double note, the skylark and its song reflected, agape and Eros. Equals and opposites. Love and hate. Calm and storm. Life and death. He sank into the bluebells. Deeper and deeper he sank until he could sink no more. The light was a blue light, soulful and shimmering. Hitler and Stalin held out their arms and starlight pierced their hands with silver nails. The guards from the concentration camps threw dice for their robes of light. The victims of the Holocaust and the Terror

51

circled this ethereal Golgotha. No more were they flesh or blood, body or bone. They were beings of light; sentient coruscations. They were sad for the potentates, the heinous perpetrators. Hitler and Stalin looked deep into each others eyes, and spoke with the tongues of angels. They knew what they had done. They knew that on earth they hadn't known who they were; who the corpses were, the tortured and the tormented. They had to choose. Redemption was death of the spirit, another incarnation, another life on the wheel, broken by suffering. They had chosen to suffer on earth, another life, another life of many. 'What you do to others, you do unto yourself'. They had to pay the price, to learn and evolve. The victims were sad. The glittering victims, bathed in a blue light, buoyant and blessed. They were free, they were higher beings. Powers and principalities, cherubim and seraphim. You will return they sang; sang with the voice of angels. You will return, you will be free like the breath of stars, like love's untold and limitless Assumptions. He was rising, up through the blue depths, up into the light. A skylark was singing. There was a faint smell. Bluebells or roses? He wasn't sure. Between the trees he could see the meadows, the sweet hay meadows. The landscape was green and white; fertility and purity. The Sacred King was lying with the Queen of May, and the may-flowering thorn wafted its fragrance on the warming air. Sweetness or corruption? He wasn't sure. His own tree; his unlucky tree.

The swifts are back. Zephyr and Flora are in communion. The west wind and the wild flowers. The wind and the wild flowers. He could hear the doves in the trees; the ring-doves, the sound of emergent summer. Peacocks and tortoiseshells sipped from the teeth of lions, the dandelions, the gold doubloons of May. Still the cuckoo sang, if you could call two notes a song. The yaffle laughed, and laughed, and laughed, as if the sun would never know a cloud. Who cleft the Devil's hoof? He didn't know. Was it life or death, spirit or material? If it was death then he would talk to the bees. The bees said it was God, God who cleft the Devil's hoof. But why, he said, why would a God wish evil. The bees were the vocal chords of flowers. He had no choice, they droned, this is the way things are; the way things have to be. Nectar and pollen he could understand, sweetness and the future, love and the love of life. Why should the bee die, the baby die; the rose shed its summer petals? The daffodils were tarnished in the borders; gold that had turned to rust. He cut off their heads, tossed them into the compost. The bees spoke again. To know life you must know death, to live you must die, to die you must live. How would God know his glory? How would he come to his glory if he were only spirit? He has to experience the temporal; life in forgetfulness. He must come to an understanding through the flesh. Must know his love afresh. Must experience the duality. Both sides of the living coin, both heavy and ethereal. The dandelions were ducats and doubloons. Peacocks and tortoiseshells sipped with the velvet angels, powdered the air with wings. He had known pain. He had suffered in the mind, had suffered in the body. He remembered screaming in agony. Night after night, day after day, screaming in agony. He remembered the intensity of pain, the unbearable pulse of pain, the loneliness of pain. He remembered the morphine, the opiate, nature's palliative. Not a cure for pain, an expedient, a release. He remembered floating. A skylark lifted into the blue beyond. Its song was like rippling water, cool and clear and soothing. He was talking to the bees. They asked him to follow them, back, back, into the centre of their hive. It was warm and sweet, but the sound was his former mind, a cacophony, a synaptic interference. He was mad and he lived with madness. The living dead haunted the wards and the corridors. He walked with them. He was another self; a doppelganger, an image of the scythe in fields of hay. He could hear children singing, fairground music. Spiders crawled across the parquet floor. Rain slanted and fell, but never moistened. Parts of his body were hot. There was fire in the centre of his being. He was Beltane, he was May-Day; he was the Sacred

King. They kept giving him drugs, more and more drugs, stronger and stronger drugs. He wanted to die, but he was already dead. He was in Hell, in Hades. Pluto and the Devil, demons and ghosts. Fire. A fire that burnt when fire shouldn't burn. There were screams, Gorgons with snakes for hair, three-headed dogs with slavering mouths; and fairground music, music and children singing. The ring-doves rounded their syllables. Summer was in the trees. Light on the leaves. Love in the balmy air. He could smell the may-flowering thorn. His tree; his unlucky tree. Thorns and blossom; sweetness and corruption. He couldn't choose, he had chosen before, if before existed. They were cutting the first hay, the sweetest hay. The scythe was slicing, backwards and forwards, across and across, backwards and forwards. A skylark hung suspended in mid-air. All was azure and gold, greenness and whiteness. The velvet angels moved from flower to flower. He had no choice; he would live, he would live forever.

The May-Queen and the Virgin Queen. Mother and Goddess, Goddess and mother. A white dove lifted into the sky on clattering wings, stopped for an eternal second in mid-flight, then glided in a spiral back to earth. He was watching the dove, he loved the doves; he always watched the doves. They were the symbols. Peace and the holy fire, love and the lilt of roses. His heart was a rose, a perfect rose, suffused with the sacred blood. The fields of golden rape rippled in the breeze, lapped at his garden fence. The swifts were cuneiform on blue papyrus, curved and contrasted in the leaching light. The light had been leached from the stars. A stellar light; a shimmering incandescence. A cuckoo was the Angelus. A resounding bell, hollow and hallowed, through the hawthorn's virgin blossom. There was a river in his mind. The year's first lilies were filling their cups with gold, and their greening palms floated in silver that was skimmed by swallows. His garden and the fields of rape, the river and the dew-ponds, the skylark's reflected song, the cuckoo's Angelus. All were the same place, all were the same time; all were timeless. Deep in the river the rape was glimmering. The skylark was gilded. The hawthorn a vestal virgin, guarding the fires of Vesta; the Beltane fires, the summer fires. Was he in his garden? Was he by the river? He wasn't sure, he couldn't know for certain. A common tern plunged through his fathoming thoughts and exploded at the river's surface. Gold was in smithereens; silver a million shards. Death was as quick as this, an unguarded moment, an eye averted from the river's liquid mirror. What could he do? What could he say? The clock was ticking, but time stood still. Was he in his room or by the river? It didn't matter, this was death; he knew it was death. What of the sparrow or this tiny fish? Did they ask? Were they told? Did they know? Instinct was the cuckoo's Angelus, a knell in the summer air, a threnody. The clock was ticking. Through the window the golden rain was losing its petals. The lilac turning brown. What could he do? What could he say? June would be rich with roses and meadowsweet; convolvulus drink the sunlight and the bees. The swifts were back. May until August. Summer personified. He sat before the screen and started to write. His words were as black as the swifts. The screen the colour of hawthorn blossom; if white could be called a colour. He remembered a rainbow in April, a spectral arc, the differences of white when it's divided. The clock was ticking, but he didn't hear it. His thoughts were somewhere else; somewhere in the glittering skyscape, somewhere where a rainbow spans a dove.

May is not always sunshine; birdsong and blossom. He decided on a pilgrimage, his regular excursion to the sea. The north sea. The cold grey winter sea. An easterly wind cut across the pewter waves, and the lowering stratus enveloped the beaches and the shivering landscape. St Peters on the Wall. An Anglo-Saxon chapel built on the ruins of a Roman fort, straddled the saltings and the littorals of time. Grey stone in the grey sky, lost and as lonely as the curlew's haunted music. Founded by St Cedd in the seventh century. Pivotal for two religions. The one God and the many. Thirteen hundred years of prayer and worship. Here by the grey sea; the northern sea, the Saxon sea. He could feel the time and the timelessness; the Nordic Gods and the God from the Middle East. He had come to this isolated place along a track between the fields of corn. The corn was neither gold nor green. The skylark's song was salted, and the shivering wind washed through the cornfields on a wave of whispers. Headlands were a flood of wild flowers. Poppies and mayweed, resplendent yet unresolved. Passion and purity. Fire and ice. Poppies and corn. Body and blood. Wine and the sun a wafer through the clouds. The trees were pillars of salt. Seagulls had wings of salt, and salt was in the sadness of their cries. One God and many. Spirits of the trees. Spirits of water. Kings of the corn. He entered the ancient chapel. Fell to his knees in front of the crucifix. How many knees have knelt in this same spot? How many prayers have echoed in this edifice of Christ? Easter was on his mind. Easter and the sun on the horizon, red and remembered like the blood of poppies. 'This is the blood of my new covenant, drink this in remembrance of me'. The One and the many. Attitudes of grey sky argue with sea for their definition, and the crying gulls worry like language in their isolation. Gulls are echoing in the chapel. Grey songs against grey stone. Time against timelessness. Hawthorn blossom flowered on the altar. A red rose floated in the chalice, a white rose in the ciborium. Body and

Blood. Christ and the Virgin Mary. Jerusalem, Jerusalem; the farmland and the black satanic mills. Innocence or experience? Birth or death? He didn't know, he wasn't sure. God was a painting by Blake; a vision, an infinite mystery. He walked out into the grey; into the grey sky, the grey sea, and the grey land. The sun was a halo, a nimbus. Misted in the grey sky, misted and turning silver. A swallow swooped in from the sea. Gathered the silver on its wings. Skimmed across the poppies and the mayweed. Wound the air on its living spool; the silver air, the quicksilver air. Chalice and ciborium, crucifix and paten. All silver. Silver like the sea. Silver like the lost and lonely gulls. Silver like his thoughts. So many ghosts. So many pilgrims. Beowulf and the Venerable Bede. Dragons to be slayed, histories to be written. The One and the many. The many and the One. St Cedd drifted in on the shivering tide. The poet prostrated himself. Caedmon was singing his sacred songs, and St Hilda was listening. The sea songs, the grey songs, the songs of a dying God. Was it birth or death? Gods were born and Gods died, but the sea; somehow eternal. He walked into the sea. The grey sea, the silver sea, the pewter sea. Neptune rose up in front of him, pointing his trident to the stars. The One and the many. Three into One. The Trinity. Venus languished in a giant oyster-shell, as pure and perfected as a galactic pearl. A blue-whale opened its ravening maw; he struggled against the

59

in-rush of the water, but to no avail. Inside the air was azure. There was a faint smell, a smell of bluebells and roses. The sunlight slanted through the whale's enormous ribs. It was like a vaulted ceiling, a subaqueous cathedral. Hawthorn petals fluttered down from the arches and the bosses, like cabbage-whites or soft forgotten feathers. A white dove was caught in the spectrum of the stained-glass windows; and a skylark was Elijah, framed in a wheel of ecstatic fire.

JUNE

Comfrey

How many shades of blue have summer skies?
As many as the comfrey by the river
Whose drooping heads turn purple to the eye -

And hang - like mist. There's even pink amongst
The varied blooms - enough it seems to haunt
The water's edge - like ghosts that learn their numbers

From the bees. The air is warm. The jaunt
Of our desire visits June - where sunlight
Flits through shadows with the wren - undaunted

In the glitter of its song. The thrush replies -
A flood of notes that fathom every flower
And saunter through the fragrance of the mind.

The cuckoo seems uncertain of its taunt
And summer - doesn't answer: only hums.

Seremonath, to the Saxons. June, the dry month. The month of the wild roses. It was his birthday month; Gemini, the twins. Castor and Pollux, two stars, doubles at the solstice when the sun stands still, when time stops. The cuckoo's double note was breaking down. Rape was turning brown and the corn becoming golden. He walked along the lane towards the church; St Nicholas Church, Canewdon. Canewdon or Canute's hill; the place where he camped before the battle of Ashingdon, before he defeated Edmund Ironsides, a Saxon, before a Dane became king of England. Dog rose and downy rose, field rose and burnet. Pale pinks, deep pinks, white and creamy white. A month before the dog star; yet hot enough, as hot as that distant battle, fought in the river valley; fought to the death under the seagulls' cries, under the sun and the salt-laden air. Hogweed and hemlock held up their umbels to the sun. White patens for the golden wafer, a refuge and succour for the soldier-beetle, looking for sweetness in his bronzed and burnished armour. The cumuli was building into blue. Glacial cloudscapes. Samuel Palmer's clouds, white uplifting clouds suffused with black, bruised with black at their soft and vaporous bases. A dragonfly threaded gold. The devil's darning needle, braiding the hedgerow; the composites, the buttercups. He had gold on his shoes. Pollen and nectar dusted the air with fragrance, and the summer warmth heated the skylark's song. Samuel

Palmer's skylark; a black and yet blazing star. St.Nicholas, patron saint of children and the depths of winter. Here in the light's midsummer, thinking of Herod and the Holy Innocents. The roses are wine and bread; body and blood. The cuckoo's song is frozen, the nightingale a corpse. Light is splayed. Is gold from the summer sun gilding the clouds and their thunderous bruises. Air is heavy and humid. Perspiration trickles down his brow; salt from the tidal river, salt from the seagulls crying. Two cabbage-whites climb and convolve, curve through the double-helix. They are at war; possessive of territory, possessive of their genetic heritage. The sun is softened, then occluded, blocked by the bruising clouds, its summer passage moistened to the point of tears. Forked light wriggles down the sky, and the Gods cackle with thunderous voices. Rain is relentless and torrential. Great drenching drops ricocheting through the leaves, forming a river in the ancient lane. He just stands there, drenched and dishevelled like the hunching doves. Sound and light, light and sound, resplendent and resounding. Perspiration from the Gods, trickling down the sky's brow, the bruised cheeks. The Dane-Geld will be the corn; will be the harvest of the battle, the cause of the war. Bread and territory; territory and bread. How much blood from the dripping roses? How much bread from the sodden flowers? 'This is the bread of the new covenant; eat this in remembrance of me'. The

63

rivulets of rain funnelled into the fields of corn. The corn was drinking, drinking the summer to its lees. Poppies and mayweed were unresolved. Wounds and bandages; blood and the broken skin. The sun returned and a skylark lifted on angelic wings. Samuel Palmer's skylark, Shelley's skylark. Vaughan-Williams and Meredith sang and ascended in the summer air. All was song and the sound of battle. The thunder rumbled somewhere in the distance. His clothes were steaming, the road was steaming. The dragonfly returned with its golden threads, braided the hogweed and the drowning hemlock; hung in its stasis, like the lark in sun-shafts.

Matins to evensong. The longest day and not a cloud to sully in the sky. These are the offices of gold. Bees are taking the sacrament, both species, nectar and pollen. He walked by the river, damascene, diaphanous and dazzling. Comfrey was in bloom; a misted cloud of whites and blues and purples. A wren astounded with the glitter of its song, and then the silence, the calm and holy silence. Lauds and prime, tierce, sext, none. Noon was a prayer, a psalm. A song-thrush sang a canticle. The litany was doubled and repeated, doubled and repeated in the trees, the green trees, the golden trees, the transpirational choirs. A swallow skimmed the silver of his thoughts. His thoughts and the season were one. Time and timelessness. Here at the river's edge, here at the solstice hour when the sun stands still, when the heavens rest and the swallows are fixed in silver. Transfixed. Cruciform above the river's glass. 'Through a glass darkly'. But now he would know in full. A golden rudd swam into the sun, the reflected sun. Gold into sunken gold. Fire in water. Fire in the mirror. The song of the wren glittered in the meridian, glittered at the zenith. Apex and acme; alpha to omega. Comfrey and loosestrife rippled in the sifting breeze. Scented and seasoned his ecstatic vision. The song of the thrush was silent. No more the doubles, the repeated phrases, the cuckoo's double dealing. And old brick bridge arched across the river. A weather-worn and mossed and lichened rainbow, spanning the river, spanning the rippling waters. He leaned across the bridge's parapet and looked into the water, the rippling sliver water. Swallows flew in and out, under the rainbow, the mossed and lichened rainbow. He spoke out aloud. Christ has died, Christ has risen, Christ will come again. The words echoed and resounded, under the bridge, the worn and weathered bridge. Traffic rumbled past behind him, but he heard nothing, only The Mystery of Faith, the questions and the answers, the echoes and the intimations. This was Wordsworth's bridge, without the city, without the spires and the domes; the factories and the black satanic mills. The great heart was nature itself. Beating in the swallow's breast, the thrush's song, the glittering wren. Mallards up-ended and dabbled for weeds. They flew and chased and landed, cut swarf from water. Drakes nearly drowned the females in their lust, held their heads beneath the water, trod in the crystal spray. Leda and the Swan. God and our mortal nature. Castor and Pollux. He was a Gemini, this was the month of his birthday. Was it birth or was it death? The heavens or the rippling silver. He didn't care, it didn't matter. He scried deep into the glass. Darkly he scried, deeply he scried. He could see the sun with a swallow at its heart. Fish twisted and turned their scales into the light, glittered like a million mirrors. He was standing on a rainbow, a worn and weathered rainbow. Substance and the insubstantial. White and divided colour. The spectrum of the meadows thick with comfrey. Blue swallows and the echoes of their wings. The vespers of the breezes through the reeds. Offices of light and golden songs.

He stood by the standing circle; the granite circle, the quartz circle. All was circles and spirals. Stone circles, crop circles, maelstroms, tornados, waterspouts, galaxies, vortices, the double-helix. What was this monument for? Why? Was it built for a change in religions? To capture moon for the wandering hunters? The sun for the settled farmers? How did they understand? The movements of the sun; the cycles of the moon? Did the ice retreat and the wild game go with it? Were they forced to work the land, struggle against the rain, the frost; the droughts? Who knows, he didn't. Would he ever know? Would anybody ever know? He could only speculate. The circle captured the sun and the moon in due season. The past and the present petrified. Did they have the need for both God and Goddess; summer and winter, day and night? A pair of cabbage-whites coiled and convolved. He placed his hand over the cup-and-ring markings. He began to tingle from head to foot. He could feel a power; a coiling power, a convolving power. He could see the Milky Way, not as a shimmering haze, but as a spiral, a diminishing spiral. The galaxies, the genetic helices, they were all the same, 'as above so below'. A hare ran into a golden field, stood on his hind legs and pricked his ears above the corn. He wasn't mad, he was never mad. According to the Hindus the hare is sacred to the moon, and to the Saxons the Kern King was the spirit of the sun. The moon and the sun are joined. Was this the reason? Was this why the stones were erected? Who knows? The poet didn't know, the hare didn't know, nor did the corn. He walked into the centre of the stone circle and held out his arms. The convolving cabbage-whites, unwound from their fluttering spirals, and settled; one in each of his hands. One turned into shimmering gold and the other to glittering silver. Artemis and Apollo.

Huntress and Shepherd. He held the moon and the sun in his human hands. A flight of golden arrows whistled above his head. Lambs were bleating in the meadows. Romantic or classical? Feeling or thought? The moon was in his left hand, the sun in his right. Sinister or dexter? Witches or wise men? Silver or gold? He didn't know, he couldn't chose, his mind was eclipsing. He moved into the stone, into the black granite, into the white quartz. The sun and the moon orbited in his thoughts, spun and spiralled, merged into the Milky way. Microcosm and macrocosm. DNA and the spiral galaxy. Distance and locality. Positions in space; positions in the mind. Light grew dim, and the stone became as black as basalt. Wild roses bloomed in his subconscious. Pink and white; pure and perfected. The blood of the Christ, the flesh of the Virgin Mary. He was entering a black hole. Gravity drew him in, and light could not escape. Only the roses, the pink and the white roses. This was singularity, only the mind of God, only the love of the Goddess. A nightingale was singing, but where was it singing? This was nowhere, not anywhere, nothing. Nothing was the song of a nightingale, the sweet melodious song, and the holy roses. He was no-one and everyone, nothing and everything. He could hear the stones, the music of the stones, the power of the stones. Cup-and-ring, maelstrom and tornado, waterspout and double-helix. His own unconscious code was the code of the stars, the galaxies. He opened his hands in the stone, the dark stone; the dazzling stone. The moon and the sun were metamorphic. A pair of cabbage-whites, coiled and convolved, blazed in the depths of stone. Light and life were winding in a spiral. Granite and quartz and basalt burst into a million shards. The sun re-entered the continuum, began to move once more. Time had been re-asserted. Love and lust would have to learn their lessons. Days in the depths of the sunlit soil; nights in the shadows of a Hunter's moon.

Hailstones as large as eggs flattened the barley, the rape-seed, and the corn. The Gods were angry and their forked tongues wriggled and cackled down the basalt sky. St Nicholas Church surmounted the hill of Canute. Grey stone, grey sky, lightning and the crash of thunder. He stood in the porch to shelter from the rain, the pummelling hailstones. A gargoyle spouted water and the drowning doves hunched in the arches of the Norman tower. The leaves on the sycamore rattled with raindrops, gathered and released the falling water. Rainwater flooded the paths and flowed out in a torrent under the dripping lych-gate. Raindrops ricocheted and reverberated. Bubbles built and burst, floated, then vanished in the humid air. Canute could not hold it back. The fathoming summer tide breached the defences and entered the inner sanctum. He waded down the centre aisle. Edmund Ironsides prostrated himself by the altar and prayed to his God for victory. Canute's God was the same God. How was a God to choose? To choose between sinners, rivals for land and riches, revenue and power. The Gods were angry. Thunderbolts and hailstones, torrential rain and lightning. St Nicholas thought of the children, Herod's children, the innocents. Why should it come to this; blood and battles, battles and blood? Man against man and children, man against the Gods? But there is only one God, one God for Ironsides; one God for Canute. Canute would be the victor. Would dedicate a churh to his God. St Andrew's Minster, on the hill at Ashingdon, overlooking the cornfields and the Tidal river. He would believe that right was on his side, he'd won the battle, and his God had given him the prizes. Ironsides would suffer, would know that he must have been wrong, that England was destined for Denmark, that his God demanded compliance. The rain began to ease and the poet took out his notebook. He would have to capture the rain, hold it in ink, save it for the future generations. He was important, the rain was important, God was important. The sun glittered in the sycamore and a wren began to sing. Along the green lane a dragonfly threaded gold amongst the hemlock. Quicksilver hung from the leaves and umbels. Dripped its inverted worlds. Gurgled along the gullies. Cascaded into the drains. A rainbow arched from the Crouch to the River Thames. A skylark climbed the spectrum; over the fields of corn, the glittering barley. Comfrey was in his mind. The horizon was blue, the cumuli white, and the rainbow a shimmering purple. He walked along the verge. The wild roses glistened like porcelain. Tears of gold dripped from their opulent petals. Was this not enough? It was free; it was there for the taking. The brambles were fruiting. The first ripening berries, both black and red, blood and a summer's bruising. He looked down from the hill, out and across the ripening cornfields, the isolated trees, the clustering copses. In the misted distance, office-blocks and towering flats, flashed in the blazing sunlight. The rainbow spanned the sadness of his thoughts, and a soaring skylark sang in the sun-shafts with the voice of a ravishing angel.

JULY

Mute Swans

The marshes were my home - the creek's eternal
Silver - and the sun - singing of summer
And the silent swans. Leda - as yet - unheard

Of: the Gods were gentle - swans had the wings
Of angels and the fleets were rich with eels
And golden rudd. Remembering such things -

Such light defined - can make me feel
The past is still alive - that summer lingers.
You'd think that - now - in honesty - was real:

The past as dead as frankincense and myrrh -
The memory - as muted - as a mummer.
But no - the swans of summer - still return -

Connecting past and present - though they're dumb -
With every myth - and moment: that reveals.

This is the hottest month. The month when the Dog-Star rises with the blazing sun, doubles the dawning and the depth of heat. He walked into the garden, looked at the balsam and the blooming roses; studied the velvet of the delving bees. The heat was intense. He took off his shirt and sat in the chair beside the pond. The air was sultry and oppressive. Sunlight blistered on his naked shoulders. Time and timelessness cauterised his mind, his unbelieving mind. Bees were drawn into the flowers, caught and cremated by the boiling nectars. The heat was unbearable. Butterflies sizzled in the air, were charred like the paper in unwelcome books. Sunlight was censorious, criticized the bowers and the cooling shade. Shadows were on fire. Hell was the conflagration, buddleia the purple fumes of Hades. He was suffering, everything was suffering. He remembered the midnight road, the speeding car and the oncoming bend. He remembered the brick-wall, the street-lamp and the moon above the rooftops, buoyant and bronzing in the violet sky. Slow down, he said, slow down. Nobody listened. There was a crash, a terrible crash. Glass was in smithereens, bricks into splinters and the shards of bone. He lay in the road uncertain of his being, uncertain of the road, uncertain of the moon above the rooftops. There was a faint smell, a smell of bluebells and roses, petrol and rubber. A woman was cradling his head, and darkness moved from his feet towards his brain. Don't let me die, he said, please don't let me die. The pain was unbearable, consciousness an impossibility. Twenty years passed; twenty slow and painful years. Were they years or were they timeless? The past or the present or the future? He didn't know; he could not be certain. He lay on the theatre trolley. Was wheeled along the corridors. Before him were the operating theatres. Three doors in a line, three doors in a clinical line. A man in a green mask gave him the anaesthetic. Anaesthetic or xyclon B. The three doors were clinical, cold and clinical, like Auschwitz, like Treblinka. The anaesthetic found its mark. There was a tremendous crash, an explosion. Glass was in smithereens, brick in a million shards. He had suffered, physically and mentally. He awoke in the recovery ward, his head in a chromium bowl, coughing and spewing. He didn't know where he was, why he was, who he was. He passed out again, was nowhere and nothing and no-one. A skylark sang in his unconscious mind. Roses bloomed; red roses, white roses. When he awoke again he was in the general ward. Through the windows the cumuli rose into the boundless blue. The cumuli was pink, pink in the evening sun, pink and uncanny, pink and frightening. All he could think of was death, death and the death of hope. He was depressed; down in the depths of terror, desolate and depressed. Nothing made sense; all was black,

black and negative. Blossom was on the trees, skylarks singing in the April air. What could he do? What could he say? How could he survive? Night came slowly with the stars and the bronzing moon. He wanted to sleep but he couldn't sleep. He was terrified of sleep, terrified of death, terrified of nightmares and oblivion. He lay there on his bed. The heat was unbearable. The sleeping-tablets hadn't worked. Night-lights glimmered. Planets wandered through his mind. Stars exploded. Shattering glass; splinters of brick and bone. Darkness moved from his feet towards his brain. An enveloping darkness, an ultimate darkness. He couldn't think, he couldn't hope. There was a faint smell, a smell of bluebells and roses, petrol and rubber. He could taste the petrol, taste the rubber. Christ was in the operating-theatre. The xyclon B permeated the atmosphere. Hitler and Stalin were holding their scalpels. Each of the scalpels glinted under the theatre lights, the hot lights, the unbearable lights. A nightingale was singing. Was this birth or death? Birdsong or threnody? A pyramid of bodies, cold and naked bodies, piled up towards the heights and the singing nightingale. But its throat was cut, cut by the scalpels and the slicing stars. Did he sleep or did he die? Red was the setting sun; red with the blood of the rose, red on the rostrum of his heart lamenting.

His lover was in the garden, smelling the roses, the

white roses, the red roses. She was lithe and blond and beautiful. But she had suffered. Suffered in the flesh; suffered in the mind. Eros or agape? Lust or love. She was a woman of the flesh, a sensual woman, an erotic woman. But she had suffered, suffered from his abstinence, his sexual abstinence. Chastity, celibacy, purity. Bees were in communion with the flowers. Peacocks and painted ladies were kissing the buddleia. He could fantasise on sex and enjoy the fantasy. Without the bees and the flowers, without man and woman, the sun would cease to exist. Life would be darkness and a shattered helix. He loved the weather, the heat. But write as he may he couldn't express the weather; it was the weather that was expressing him. He was the sun, the bee, the flower. Body or spirit? He loved this woman dearly. She was the weather, the sunlight through the leaves, the blackbird's summer song, the rainbow and the skylark cast in gold. He had enjoyed the flesh, their flesh, their mortal flesh. But it was not enough, far from enough. His love was in the mind, the heart, the spirit. He knew that she loved him; he knew that he loved her. Despite the differences, the dilemmas, they were still one. They thought for each other, loved each other; lived for each other. He had known her before she was born; he will know her after she dies. She is the rose, he is the delving bee. Union, communion, consummation. The honeysuckle twined along the garden fence.

The fragrance drew them together, the beauty was entrancing, captivating. They looked into their each observing eyes, saw starlight and roses, white doves, larkspur and lilies. Why did the black rose have to bloom in her perfect body? Why was love a growing canker? Time is the sword of Damocles. Cancer the hair that holds it over life. Who suffers most? The bee suffers for the shrike, the butcher bird. Is impaled on a thorn to die, devoured and digested. The fly is trapped in silk, poisoned by gossamer, wrapped in a shimmering shroud. The sparrow suffers because of the hawk; the seed suffers because of the sparrow. Who suffers most? He knew that it must be God. God is everything, everything is God. God is the eternal sacrifice, victim and victor. The cross proves it. The cross in the heat of Golgotha, The cross on the hill of skulls. God suffered for the world; suffered for the sake of Love. They live for the day, two people in one mind. Two bodies in one flesh. They are soul mates, they can never leave each other. They are the sentiments of the stars; spirits of water, earth and air and fire. There is a faint smell, a smell of petrol and bluebells, clinical wards and disinfectant. The moon is a white rose, a yellow rose, blooming over the summer rooftops. A brick-wall and a speeding car come together in the name of death, but he doesn't die. Starlight glitters in basalt. Each single star a cell, an integral part of love and the living galaxies. Black stars multiply, spread darkness through the astral bodies; the light bodies. Christ holds out his arms, life in one hand; death in the other. He is both life and death; death and life. The cuckoo's double song has died, the nightingale is singing. He walks towards his lover and the roses. Their lips touch in the moonlight. A pipistrelle hoards silver on its holy wings, and the scented stocks revive the moths with reveries and nectars.

What is poetry? Music, meaning, association? How can it deal with the heat, the July heat, the Dog Star and the lifting sun? The heat is a searing heat. A fire-storm through the trees. A laying waste of the grasses and the meadowsweet. The cumulus is billowing, a fungal cloud; a mushroom cloud. The heat is Hiroshima; Nagasaki. The heat is napalm; a shroud of fire. A running girl in a shroud of fire; a naked girl, a screaming girl. Grasshoppers stridulate. A monotonous and melancholy music. What does it mean? What does it mean for the fire in the leaves, the scorched grass; the cremated corpses? A pair of cabbage-whites describe a double-helix in the air. They will burn if they touch the sun, the nuclear sun. They are images of Icarus, images of aspiration, of ambition. The forests are burning. People are wearing necklaces of fire. The crystal tigers are melting; melting. What could he do? What could he say? He wrote about the seasons, the cycles of the seasons, the cycles of our lives, the correspondences. But the heat, the July heat. The Dog Star and the devils made of dust. His words were fragile; burnt leaves, charred paper, crumbling petals. Thistledown drifted like the ghost of the winter snows. Fire and ice; ice and fire. He was dumb in the light of ages. The ghosts on the summer trains, the cattle trains. The Star of David, the golden star, the star of the singing psalms. 'In the valley of the shadow of death'. What could he say? What could he do? The burning centre of a star, the roaring ovens, the nuclear ovens, the smell of the burning flesh. Music or meaning or associations? What does it matter? Why should he think, why should he feel, why should he write? 'How could you believe in God after this'? 'How could you not believe in God after this'? And so it goes on, the full stop, the blemish in the eye of beauty, the finality of truth. A velvet angel buzzed and bumbled on the lips of balsam. Entered in, into communion with the flower, into the heart of being. The bee was transcendental. He didn't think, he didn't know, he didn't care; he just was. The bee the flower and the sun. The shrike did not concern him, the thorn was blunted. The sparrow was unconscious of the hawk, the talons and the tearing beak. The fly was trapped in amber, the amber of its own purported being. All was an illusion and appearances. Time had stopped in the heat; the July heat, the augmented heat, deepened and doubled by the Dog

Star rising. It didn't matter, nothing mattered. He was never born, so he couldn't die. Death was of the flesh not of the spirit. History was a fly in amber. A captured moment; a crystal moment. A pale-clouded-yellow fluttered like the Star of David; ephemeral, yet timeless. Pain was a passing dream, reality was elsewhere; glory was assured. He wrote as he had never written before. Nature was important, love was important, God was important. They were all the same, dream and reality, reality and dream. Two sides of the ethereal coin, the passing and the everlasting. He saw more than the shadows flickering on the wall of the cave. He was bathed in light, heat and enveloping light. The collared-doves drowsed in the listless trees. A pair of cabbage-whites coiled and convolved in a glittering double spiral. He was pen and paper; paper and pen. A swallow skimmed through the compass of his warming thoughts; and his shimmering lover, looked up from the roses, with her eyes on fire.

Pain and pleasure; pleasure and pain. Each supposes the other. Everything comes in twos. The cuckoo's song, a face in the river's glass, the thrush's sweet reprise, angel's wings, hands in the act of giving. The trinity is the dialectic. God the thesis, Christ the antithesis, and the Holy Ghost the fire of higher synthesis. Life can be transcended; death can be transcended. The flower and the seed;

the seed and the flower. July, the hottest month, the golden month, the month of the Dog Star and the perfect rose. Dusk came slowly, warm and calm, and moonlit. The moon was over the corn, the blown moon, the perfect moon. Gold was touched with silver. A nightjar chirred. An owl hooted. The swifts were flying upwards, higher and higher, up into silence and the leaching starlight. Warmth or coldness; coldness or warmth. A cat emerged from the corn, and two electric eyes glared in the fading light. His footsteps were as light as whispers as he followed his moon-shadow over the straddling bridge and down to the river's margins. He found a swim he fancied, settled down and set up his tackle. He sprinkled some ground-bait over the water and the shattered surface rippled with shards of silver. The swallows had gone to roost and the bats had taken their place. Loosestrife was purple smoke in a silver fire. A hare ran up beside him, sat stock-still; was petrified in silver. He cast his bait into the river, put the rod in its rest, and settled back in warm anticipation. Love and hate. Good and evil. Life and death. Everything in twos; duality. There was no other way; how could it be otherwise? However it was in the spirit world, here there were equals and opposites. Schisms and dilemmas; divisions and duplicity. His bite detector started to buzz. He held the rod in both hands and struck. The rod bent double and line was screaming outwards from the reel. He adjusted the clutch and began to play the fish. It was a big fish, a heavy fish, slow but powerful. Eventually it surfaced, turned its golden flank, and then submerged, back into the glittering silver. Silver and gold; gold and silver. It was a bream, a bronze bream, seven or eight pounds in weight. An owl hooted, and another owl replied. The bream surfaced again; the colour of corn, touched by the silver moon. Apollo and Artemis. Logic and intuition. He was connected by the line, connected to another world. A primal world, an instinctive world, a realm of the deep subconscious. He was silvered by the moon, the quicksilver moon, the hunter's moon. He didn't need Hegel or Marx, Freud or Jung. Dialectics, archetypes, complexes. It didn't matter, nothing mattered. Nietzsche was dead, God was alive. Sartre was too much alone, too much himself. Here was connectedness. A fish and the hand and the moon; all in alignment, thoughtless yet all-knowing. Transcendence was the corn, the golden corn, the silver corn. The fish came slowly to the net, its glittering scales burnished and blessed in the rippling silver. The moon was a rose, a double rose, deep in the water and deep in the violet heavens. Planets wandered through the oceans of the sky, their steady light cooling and countered by stars in the tremor of their iridescence. It was July; the hottest month. Light was gathering in the east. Soon the sun would be rising; rising with the Dog Star, doubling the heat of the day. He packed his tackle away, put his bag over his shoulder and began to walk along the tow-path. He crossed the straddling bridge, the rainbow bridge, spectral in the sun's first rays. Swallows and swifts swooped and curved across the fields of corn. A blackbird was singing in the alders, its golden bill open and fluting, like the pipes of Pan. Was this birth or was it death? He didn't know, he didn't care. The moon was fading in the west. Artemis and Apollo. Huntress and Poet. He was going home, home to his bed and sleep. The moon and the sun would be always with him, deep in his drowning dreams, deep in the waters of Hippocrene.

AUGUST

Mother Earth

Nipplewort I think: strange word - a composite -
Not milky like its kin. The flower-heads -
Thin clusters in the sun - have had to fight

For energy and air. It's the same
For everyone - light is illusive - comes
When you least expect it. They seem to flame -

A beacon to the bees - who gently hum
As summer sucks its fill - dries out the dame.
Something rounds the apples and the plums -

Residues of water climb the heights
And turn all things to sweetness - out of sour.
The womb is full - the birth canal - not tight -

Nativity is nature's other name
And nipplewort - though milk-less: still succumbs.

Lammas. First fruits. Loaf-mass. He thought that July had been hot - the hottest month - but August was even hotter. First fruits and then harvest. The corn was molten gold. Corn buntings jangled their keys in the heat and the yellowhammers sang their summer songs. He was walking along a public footpath between two fields of corn, two golden fields of corn. He was the Kern King, the spirit of the sun, the spirit of harvest. Music, meaning or association. Which was the most important? The major aspect of a poem? He'd listened to what the psychologists had to say. We see in patterns; we think in associations. When you see the golden corn the mind doesn't register it as such. Notions of gold, of bread, of the heat and the summer, the body of Christ and the ears of the corn, the rabbits and the hares. All these things and more pervade the mind. And then it clicks, you know what it is, it is corn. Stalks of corn, sheaves of corn, golden corn. This was the way the mind works. A poem should re-enact the process, should be rich with associations. Then the reader would feel, feel as though they'd thought it for themselves. We think in patterns, the more patterns there are the greater seems the significance. The more important the words. The yellowhammer sang its summer song. Music, yes music, music was important. But meaning, did it matter, was there any meaning? Wasn't sentience enough, feeling, intuition, association? The bunting repeated its phrases in the heat, the unbearable heat. Couplets, stanzas, villanelles. It was England's hottest day since records began. 101 in the shade, the scorching shade. What did it mean? What did it matter? The swifts had gone. Had travelled south, into the deeper heat, the dazzling heat. Swallows rested on the wires. Their red throats burnt by the sun; their blue backs tempered by the sun, the burnishing sun. The combine harvester moved along the edges of the field in a cloud of dust and chaff. Chaffinches were forming flocks, autumn flocks, winter flocks. What did it mean? What did it matter? Questions and resolutions. The sun was a sonnet, a shimmering sonnet. The swallows twittered. Anapaests and iambics, trochees and dactyls. What did it mean? What did it matter? He wasn't sure; he didn't know. The cuckoo's double note was somewhere else; deep in the south, the dazzling south. The swifts were gone and the doves were drowsing. Drowsing through their deep syllabics, their listless song, their summer threnody. He walked into the shadows of the hedgerow. A speckled-wood fluttered between the shade and the sun-shafts. Brown and speckled white, a pattern, an association. The brown earth dappled with sunlight, dappled with meaning. But what did it mean? He couldn't say, he wasn't certain. All was prosody, rhyme and reason, senses and associations. It was the hottest day on record. 101 in the shade, the dazzling shade. Darkness was non-existent; all was poetry, Heraclitus and Apollo, fire and lyricism. He was in the shade, the blistering shade. Perspiration trickled down his face in beads of crystal; inflammable crystal. Inverted worlds, glittering worlds; worlds on the slopes of Parnassus. The corn was gold, Apollo was gold, love was a possibility; light was a certainty. It was 101 degrees, the hottest day on record. He lay back against the trunk of an elm, a towering elm. Sunlight was sifted and scattered by the leaves, as a yellowhammer wheezed its final note. Silence and the syllabic doves; cabbage-whites, and closure.

Harvest-time; harvest and love's fruition. Gone are the lusts of spring; things are calmer now, have mellowed and are more mature. This is the time of the spirit, of the heart, of completion. His lover was with him, with him in the church. Was this a sin? He wasn't married, didn't want to be married. Summer's bountiful produce was laid out before the altar. Apples and pears, plums and damsons, bread and sheaves of corn. Time and place and atmosphere, this was all he wanted, all he had hoped for. The moment of harvest, the moment of death, the moment of eternity. He took communion, the bread of death, the bread of life. His lover was not confirmed, so she bowed her head, and accepted a blessing. The priest knew that they were not married. Did he care? Did it matter?

Their love was beyond all solemnization. It was love in the sight of God; God in the sight of love. Harvest and love, true love, the love of the spirit. The organ was playing. Hymns were being sung. He held his lover's hand, middle-aged and still holding hands. The sonorous notes of the organ echoed through the chancel and the nave. A large red crucifix, hanging on a chain from the vaulted ceiling, swung gently in the air's unsung vibrations. Sunlight splayed through the stained-glass windows, and a rainbow on the floor remembered April. There were birds on the stained-glass windows. Blackbirds and thrushes, linnets and skylarks. Christ was reborn in April. Love was renewed in April. April was light and the legacy of love. He remembered a daffodil, a Lent-lily. One lone daffodil, out of place and alone, deep in the snows of January. Herrick's daffodil, Herrick's eternal spring. 'Intimations of immortality', Wordsworth's daffodils before they lost their heads. Kings lost their heads, queens lost their heads; the aristocracy lost their heads. Wordsworth knew the answer in spite of his radical youth. Romanticism transcended reality, what ever reality is. God is the answer, and only God. God in the seed, God in the growing corn, God in the harvest wafer. He looked up at the swinging crucifix, and began to drift, to dream. Hlafmaesse. Loaf-mass. Latin mass. Saxon Mass. St Cedd floated in from the east, from the northern sea, the grey sea, the pewter sea. He floated in through the stained-glass windows. His halo was the sun and the moon, and he was surrounded by singing angels. The Pope was on his knees; the Archbishop of Canterbury was on his knees. Schisms were forgotten. Gay priests were forgotten. Women priests were forgotten. Adultery was forgotten. Sin was forgotten. All was love and the light of love. A white dove levitated in the sonorous air, the musical air. He looked at his lover and she smiled. The smile was a rose, a red rose, a mystical rose. The offerings by the altar were illuminated. Bread; golden bread. Bread for the hungry, bread for Africa, bread for China, bread for the witch-doctor, bread for the commissar. All was loaves and fishes, sunlight and symbols. 'Blessed are the poor in spirit; the meek will inherit the earth'. All was beauty and beatitudes, blessings and the fruits of the earth. He stood up, held his lover's hand, and floated along the centre aisle. They went out through the door, the arching door, the rainbow door. Horse-chestnuts were hanging in the trees. Green and golden; green and illuminated. The ring-doves dropped their syllables of sound, summer sound. Roses bloomed along the churchyard wall. Red roses, white roses, golden roses. Bread and wine, body and flesh, sunlight and the holy fire. Buses and lorries, cars and pedestrians, a police siren, an ambulance siren. He didn't hear them, she didn't hear them. They were in love, in love with

God, in love with each other. A skylark was a black star hanging in the vibrant heavens. The sun was nimbus in a shimmering gauze of cloud, a shimmering sheet of blue and feathery cirrus. A skylark spiralled into the sun, the glittering sun, the resplendent sun. Skylark and Apollo, into the sun, into the vortices; the golden and glorious vortices. The Milky Way spun on its axis, its ethereal centre. The lovers were transported. Higher and higher; deeper and deeper. Macrocosm or Microcosm? They didn't know, they didn't care. Galaxies were in their minds; their minds were in the galaxies. She was his mother, his lover, his sister, his daughter. God and Goddess. Artemis and Apollo. Huntress and Poet. Moonlight and sunlight; glimmering, glittering, resplendent and endless. They hung in the heavens, like a gold and silver song. Shimmering, shimmering, like the wings of skylarks.

He stood in the centre of his garden. Between the doves and the death of daffodils; the blackbird and the blistering roes-hips. How did they all evolve, if evolution is the word? How were they created, if creation is the word. He didn't know, he wasn't sure. 'In the beginning there was the Word, and then there was light'. He was plucking a rose for his beloved. He scratched his arm on a thorn. Blood was trickling down his arm, beads of blood, blisters of blood. The blood thickened and coagulated. He had been told that for this to happen the blood must contain innumerable chemicals all working in unison. Just one chemical missing and his blood would not have coagulated. What did this mean? How could such a combination come about by natural selection? Just one chemical missing and he would have bled to death. How could such a system evolve? All must be there from the start; every nuance, each necessity. What did it mean? He didn't know, he wasn't sure. God was a thought, and what he thought he created. Thinking must be the answer, not blind chance, not even blind faith. But thinking stopped him from feeling, took him further away from the centre. He thought of embryos, chicken embryos, fish embryos, human embryos. They all look alike, and yet they change through time, differentiate, become dissimilar. Is this not evolution? He didn't know, he wasn't sure. The air was unstable, thermals were rising, cumuli evolving. The swifts had gone, the cuckoos had gone. Spring was dead; summer was ending. What could he do? What could he say? Doves were a dirge in the trees. The greenfinch a lamentation. The droning bees a threnody. Raindrops were created out of air, substance from the insubstantial. Lightning forked; thunder coughed and cackled. The Gods were angry. We didn't believe them. We believed ourselves, our knowledge and our science. We'd forgotten the angels, the shining ones. We didn't believe in Annunciations, Incarnations or Assumptions. God was dead, the Virgin was dead, and hope was dying. He held out his arms and the blackbirds nailed him to the meridian. Was he a God? Was he a scarecrow? Was he a thief? Who had betrayed him? He had betrayed himself, betrayed himself with doubt. 'In the beginning there was the Word, and then there was light'. He thought of a dove, and it was manifest. He thought of rose, and it bloomed beyond his mind. Creation or evolution? He didn't know, he wasn't sure. Darkness occurred at noon. April was in his mind. The tomb was open before him, and daylight was streaming into his eyes. He thought of the Trinity; the Trinity of womanhood, and three silver Goddesses appeared before him in the light. Was this an epiphany or an evolution? The Dove of fire settled on the Hill of Skulls. Daffodils bloomed in Gethsemane, and the risen sun was tall and transfigured, like a golden throne.

August was coming to an end. Summer was coming to an end. Thistledown and spidery threads floated on the rising air. Plums hung like rubies from the fingers of the trees. Pears were golden rings on the hands of leaves, and greengages, gleamed and glistened like polished jade. All was treasure, treasure was all. This was the culmination. The fruiting time, the succulent time, the time of sweetness and of fermentation. Wasps were drunk on the oozing juices. Starlings staggered. All was light and inebriation; blessed and bacchanalian. 'In vino veritas' Truth in the berries of elder, truth in the bloom of sloes, truth in the glistening grapes. He breathed in and took his fill. This was what his life had been for; conception to consummation, alpha to omega. The swallows were on the wires, they had been fulfilled. The curlew flew and fluted across the downs and out towards the marshes and the mudflats, they had been fulfilled. He was nowhere and everywhere; in time and out of time. This was summer's envoi, its epilogue, its coda. His was picking blackberries in his garden, on the downs, and by the river. The brambles were burning bushes, blood and thorns, wasps and metallic flies. He could smell the hedgerows. The traveller's joy was growing its beard, wild hops hung like golden lanterns, and the rosebay flossed and fired in the shadows. He was drunk, drunk on light, drunk on love, drunk as the doves delivered their songs of gold. He was out at sea, playing a bass, a silver bass - a bass like a thousand mirrors. Gulls screamed and circled overhead. White sails slanted to the far horizons, then disappeared into the haze. He was by the river; he was playing a golden rudd, a glittering rudd with rubies instead of fins. Purple loosestrife smoked from the shaded margins. Swallows skimmed the water's surface, shattered the glass; shattered their vitreous images. Coots bickered, moorhens ticked like clockwork, terns dived and dissembled, warblers wound their ratchets in the reeds. A pair of cabbage-whites coiled and convolved as they rose in a double spiral. Small waves were lapping against the beach. White sussurations, whispers, prayers. He was in his garden, under the chestnut, under the whispering poplar. Bees droned. Wasps were drunk on fermenting fruits. Starlings staggered. Seeds on the balsam were exploding, scattering God's shrapnel, bombarding the poppies with new life, forgetful of remembrance. Was it birth or death? He didn't know; he wasn't sure. Spring and summer combined. Conception, communion, consummation. He looked at the white roses, the roses with love's nomenclature; the roses with the name of Peace. Hawthorn blossomed in his mind. The May Queen danced around the Maypole. The Sacred King bourgeoned with buds and exploding leaves. He put a plum to his parched lips and sucked. The juices were sweet, sweet and fermenting. He was a wasp without a sting, a starling without a beak. He staggered back indoors. The clock was ticking, but time had stopped. He turned on the television. England were playing South Africa at cricket. The bowler, bowled, and the batsman struck. The ball stopped in mid-air, turned black. A swift over the savannah, a swift in stasis, a swift between two seasons. Two worlds, divided, yet not dissimilar.

SEPTEMBER

September Morning

This morning is northeasterly - and
Cirrus - where blue between the meaning of
The sky - divides in two with one long strand

Of vapour. The aircraft moves through silence
On its journey - from where to where I do
Not need to know - as journeys - in a sense -

Are what we are. Perhaps we had to choose -
But now forget - the purpose and the plan
In that one reason - that rounds the plum and bruises

All the sloes. Listen - to the robin - that's enough -
Is all you need of temperament and tense
To know - the muted odyssey - of love.

There is in this chill morning - drenched with dew -
A destination - you - can understand.

September and the first mists. Mornings of purple and gold, and the spiders' glint geometries. Convolvulus still sucks in the bees, the vibrating chords of Gabriel's scented horn. A thrush, a dove and a blackbird sit in the shimmering leaf-light. Meshach, Shadrach and Abegnego, survivors from the blistering fires of August. His garden is paradise. Dew on the lawn like a cache of diamonds. The golden eyes of the common daisy, and the seeds of balsam still exploding in his mind. He was sat at the garden table drinking his coffee. On the table were an A4 refill note-pad, a black biro, and a dictionary. He was going to write about the weather, or was the weather going to write him? He didn't know, he wasn't sure. The dove still sang its summer song, but the air was becoming chill. Shadows were longer now, and the robin's doleful song, portentous of autumn. How could he write about mist, what could he say? The mist had formed like words, substance from the insubstantial, symbols and images deep from the depths of consciousness. Dew-point, the time when the invisible is manifest. When invisible vapours condense, when nothing becomes something. The first leaves were turning; red and gold and brown. Brown like the chattering sparrows. Gold like the finches on the thistles. Red like the robin's breast. Some of the roses were tarnished, their rusty petals, falling through the mist, settling on the diamond dew-drops. The spiders' webs were vortices, glittering vortices; geometries of silver. He couldn't write and yet he felt as though he'd already written. The weather had written him. His blood was diamonded, diamonded with dew-drops. His retina was misted, was the mist itself. Spiders spun silver threads across his synapses. A thrush, a dove, and a blackbird. Meshach, Shadrach and Abegnego, a choir in the furnace of the leaves. Protected by God, protected by Heraclitus; by forms and philosophies. Shadows were flickering in his mind's cave. Shadows and forms; forms and shadows. The dew was in his mind. Mist was in his mind. The spider's glittering threads were in his mind. Were they only in his mind; did anything exist beyond his mind? He didn't know, he wasn't sure. Forms and shadows; shadows and forms. What could he do? What could he say? The robin whistled its song, its muted and melancholy song. A leaf or two sidled down the misted air, like a glittering mosaic. Red and gold; yellow and brown. He picked up his pen, his black pen, his transparent pen. The ink had turned to gold. It was sunlight and goldfinches, leaves and leaf-light. But it wouldn't write, it was already written. The rose petals, the tarnished rose petals, lifted from the diamonded dew, the misted dew. They levitated. Turned red and white. Shimmered and coruscated. They were sentient beings; beings of light. They were Hitler and Stalin. Body and blood. Bread and wine. 'Christ have mercy on us, Lord have mercy on us, Christ have mercy on us'. Blood glittered like tears. The body was tormented, charred and tormented. The Blessed Virgin was purple, purple and gold, purple and azure. She gathered the roses in her hands, hands like the whitest lilies. The roses had known the Devil; torture and torment, pain and suffering. The roses were the potentates, the perpetrators, the heinous perpetrators. They were bathed in purple, purple and gold, purple and azure. They were sentient beings, light beings, and they knew their crimes, their inhumanity. She was teaching them peace, peace and purity, charity and chastity. 'The greatest of these is charity'. It was the first mist of autumn. Meshach, Shadrach and Abegnego, sang in the funace of the leaves. Survivors of tyranny, tyranny and power. Droplets of mist were diamonded on the spiders' glint geometries. The robin's song was Keatsian; a joy, a melancholy joy. He finished his cup of coffee, picked up his pen and note-pad, and walked towards the door. The blackbird started to sing again, its golden bill opening and closing, trembling with song. He closed the door behind him. The clock was ticking, ticking, ticking, but he didn't hear it. He looked at the empty sheet of paper and sighed. The poem was written; the poem had written itself.

The Canada geese were flying low above the river. Flying and cacophonous. The air was still, so still.

Their raucousness shattered the atmosphere, and the sporadic rise of fish shattered the river's mirror. It was the Gerst-monath, the Halig-monath; the barley month, the holy month. The seventh month from March, from the time when time was different, when March was the beginning, when spring was the beginning. But now his thoughts were of autumn, the cold and the coming autumn. The Canada geese were ice, deities of ice, Gods of the crystal future. Toadflax glimmered in the verge, pallid candles, candles at the end of summer. He walked amongst the glimmering candles, and was cooled by their September heat. A bee droned amongst the candles, covered the candles; snuffed the candles. The nectars were cold, cold and sweet. They would be stored for winter, deep in the warmth of the hive; the honeycomb. A few late butterflies flickered like fire, flurried like snow. They were a kaleidoscope in blue glass, the airs blue and brittle glass. There were angels on the river's surface. Where the invisible hands of the breeze stirred at the still transparency, angels appeared, angels shimmered. The geese had settled on a lake, a lake beside the river. They were silent at last, everything was silent. This is where God is, he thought, here in the silence, the still September silence. The river was an icon. An inverted icon. Trees in their turning colours hung upside down in the glittering mirror. Everything was doubled, doubled and delineated.

The icon was sharp, clear cut, and crystalline. He looked into the mirror and he could see the face of God. This was not hubris, human pride. He knew that he was God, that everything was God. The seams of silver fish were God. The gibbous moon, the white reflected skull in the azure, was God, all was God. Why wouldn't they believe, the scientists, the philosophers, even the theologians? Nobody it seemed believed, only he believed, and nobody else believed him. The river was full of reflections, a Pandora's Box of reflections. The breezes skittered across the surface. The river was bleared. Only hope was left; hope and the silent geese, the deities of ice, the Gods of the healing crystals. There was a lull, the breeze died back, and stillness returned to haunt him. He was scrying the glass. There were ghosts in the glass. Ghosts of the past, ghosts of the present, and ghosts of the future. Time did not exist; all time was ghosted in the icon, the shimmering icon. History was in the icon; all the illusions of history were in the icon. Nietzsche had killed God. Darwin had killed God. But God was alive; he could see God, God in his own image. The tree of paradise, budded and bloomed, blossomed and fruited, above the river. Adam and Eve gazed longingly at the fruits, the fruits of unlimited knowledge. A golden apple teetered between weightlessness and gravity. He watched it with infinite fascination. Suddenly, suddenly, and for no apparent reason it fell. It hit the icon, shattered the icon. Slowly the water stilled, stilled and settled. Images were kaleidoscopic, a mosaic. Red leaves, golden leaves, brown leaves. The pieces came together, gradually, slowly and imperceptibly. A face was beginning to form, a holy face, a grave face, Newton's, cold and mechanistic face.

He was fishing for mullet on Two Tree Island. He was between Southend and Canvey, between the mudflats and the open sea. Curlew flew over his head and out towards the saltings. He could hear their cries, their plaintive and plangent cries. The first of the brent geese had arrived from Arctic Russia and Siberia. He had been watching the eel-grass for months. Their main food would be plentiful. Their skeins would be long and lingering, over the mudflats, over the saltings, over the Hadleigh marshes. The tide was almost full, almost slack. He was hiding in the bushes. A shoal of mullet shimmered in the glittering water. They ranged between two and eight pounds, he thought. He was using freshwater tackle, very small hooks, and bacon-fat for bait. Mullet have large lips, delicate lips. Large hooks were useless. If you lip-hooked them, the lips would come away, and the fish would be lost. They had to be hooked inside the mouth, on the roof of the mouth, on the inside of the cheeks, anywhere where the flesh was solid. He cast his float into the slack water and sat back.

Behind him was the old tip, no longer used, and left to the devices of nature. Giant hogweed grew in abundance. Now it was leafless, flowerless, stark and brown and skeletal. It was one of those warm September days, still and warm, and humid. A skylark tried its song, hung like a black star in the calm azure, falling and rising, rising and falling. The hogweed was skeletal, stark and skeletal in the warm azure, the calm azure, with the skylark alive and singing. Was this birth or death? He didn't know, he wasn't sure. His float, trembled, dipped, and slanted beneath the tide. He struck. The rod bent double, and the line screamed off from his reel. He adjusted the clutch and started the play the fish. He estimated it to weigh about seven or eight pounds. It fought well. Three times he had got it close to the landing-net, and three times it had turned, moved its muscular tail-fin from side to side, and submerged back into the silted depths. It was a silver fish, a glittering silver fish. It came up again about twenty feet away from him, crashed and splashed on the surface, the silver surface, the glittering surface. An explosion of crystal spray scattered in all directions. Light was reflected and refracted. A spectrum materialised, a rainbow from nowhere, the invisible made visible. He and the fish were one. His eyes were impacted silver, silver and iridescence, sunlight and crystal spray. Finally the fish came to the waiting net. It was one of those late September days, warm and calm an still. He held the fish in his two hands. It was a paten. The sun was a holy wafer. It was one of the five fishes. One of Christ's promises. Food for the heavenly feast. A curlew fluted, solemn and solitary. Brent geese unravelled their black skeins, September's longhand, written in blue, sentences in azure. He made his way across the bridge, the rainbow bridge, the spectral bridge. His shadow went on before him, a golden shadow; a dazzling shadow. A seagull curved across its own sea-salted voice, the buildings on the distant foreshore shimmered in a lactic haze, and a flock of starlings hung in the sun-shafts, like exhausted photons.

Michaelmas. The feast of St Michael and All Angels. The dragon slayer; the slayer of the Old Religion. He had killed his mother, he had killed his father and he was blinded by righteousness. They built their temples on the hills, the Pagan hills, the sacred hills. They tortured the heretics, murdered the heretics, the holy heretics. Albigenses and Cathars. Worshippers of Sophia, the Christ, the Anointed One. Keepers of the flaming silver cross, the cross between the spirit and incarnation. They murdered the Gnostics, were afraid of gnosis, universal gnosis, the loss of power. Ecclesiastical power; secular power. The leaves were turning red, turning red on the cherry. The cherry was in the mist. Suffused with blood; stained with blood. Leaves began to fall. Trickles of blood; splashes of blood. 'This is the blood of the new covenant, drink this in remembrance of me'. God and the Devil co-eternal. Was it true? Could it be? A robin started to sing. A lament; a dirge, a threnody. Why was its song so sad, so sad and melancholic? He remembered the church of his youth; St Michael's Church, high on a hill above the marshes. He remembered the elms and the rooks, the revelling rooks, the roistering rooks. He remembered the chack of the jackdaws, the tinny chack, the metallic chack. He'd been to weddings in this church, christenings and burials. Was it birth or death? He didn't know, he wasn't certain. Was it now or was it then? How could he know? How could he be sure? The rooks were purpled, purpled like the statues in Lent. The jackdaws were silver-headed, silver like the chalice, the ciborium, the paten. There was a mist across the marshes. A white mist, a ghostly mist, over the dykes, the reed-whispering fleets. Peewits climbed and curved and dived, their high-pitched double-note, faint like the cuckoos of remembered springs. He was walking across the marshes, walking towards the sea, the eternal sea. A pair of swans, mythic swans, trod water with their webbed-feet, their urgent feet. Water was swarf, crystal spray, rainbows. They lifted into the air, the blue and misted air. White and azure, white and blue, white and silver. Their wings made a ringing sound. The sound of the Angelus. A holy sound.

'Mother of God pray for us sinners now, and at the hour of our death'. Was this birth or death? He didn't know; he could not be certain. Dusk was coming in and the mist was thickening. Venus glittered in the west, the violet west; the misted west. Fire was over the marshes. Ignis fatuus, Willow-the-Wisp, Jack-o-Lantern. Ghosts from the past, ghosts of the present, ghosts of the future. Religious ghosts, secular ghosts. Albigenses and Cathars. Fascists and communists. The Goddess was a ghost; the Virgin Mary was a ghost. A silver moon; a silver rose. An owl hooted, a fox barked, and he was alone, alone and desolate. The moon was dilating, hot and expanding in the violet heavens. It was silver, quicksilver, molten silver. He was showered with moonlight, drenched with moonlight. He was in the moon, the centre of the silver and fluid moon. There was a curlew in his mind. A lonely fluting curlew, a lost soul, a wandering ghost. He was Jack-o-Lantern, Willow-the-Wisp, Ignis fatuus. He was a Cathar and a Nazi, a God and a Devil. He had tortured and murdered, had been tortured and murdered. He could hear the rooks, the roisterous and revelling rooks. They didn't care, nothing mattered. He closed his eyes in the moon, the hot moon, the fluid moon, the molten moon. The Goddess was a spider, a silver spider, and he was trapped, trapped in her steely gossamers. All was diamonded with light, diamonded with dew. It was an early

September morning, a morning of purple and gold, purple and silver. He was in his garden, shrinking - shrinking. He was moving towards the spider's glint geometry. A wasp was eating a fly, stealing the spider's staple. Tiny droplets of condensed air dripped from the radiating web. He was small enough to catch one. He was holding the moon, holding the Goddess in his hands. Was this birth or death? He didn't know, he wasn't sure. Was this the moon he held in his hands, a glittering tear, a silver pearl? The Pope was on his knees, Hitler was on his knees, Stalin was on his knees and the poet was on his knees. He was still shrinking - shrinking - shrinking. He was a particle, a wave, pure energy, a thought. A thought in the mind of God. All was galaxies and vortices, helices and spirals. A pair of cabbage-whites, coiled and convolved, with frost on their summer wings. Was this birth or was it death? He wasn't sure, he could not be certain.

OCTOBER

Dead Leaves and Crocuses

Don't be confused - the sun will shine tomorrow
Just the same - the starlings murmur something
Of the truth. I know you've seen the swallows

On the wires - but they'll return with summer
On their wings - to dive across the dazzle
Of a lake. Nicodemus - summoned

All his nerve - and put the selfsame puzzle
To a God: a God who never dumb -
Who was the Word - said even gold can nuzzle

Through the earth. Rebirth - my friend - will follow
This dead leaf: as sure as hope and spring
Are unconfined - your grave is shallow.

Think not of death - as seeds - imbibe the drizzle -
The creed you know - will raise you: from the tomb.

The wood was a wondrous place. Splayed light fathomed the misted air. It was a golden world, golden leaves and mist, grey suffused with gold. Acorns were pattering on the ground; sound amongst the soft and October silence. A squirrel was a silver wave; an oscillation through the branches. Jays flew backwards and forwards, collecting the acorns, making a store for winter. The jays were exotic; pink and white and azure, out of place and yet somehow at home in the gold and striated greyness. Fungi were pushing through the mould, through the grass, and clinging to wood, dead and decaying wood. Jew's ear and polypores, blewits and fly agaric, death cap and boletus. The fly agaric were fairy toadstools, elvestools, gnome-stools. Red and white spotted, unwholesome and hallucinatory. He pinched a speck of the red flesh and put it in his mouth. He knew that it was dangerous, that it contained alkaloids, was poisonous. But the Vikings had used it, the Berserkers had used it. He wondered if the warriors of Canute had used it at the battle of Ashingdon. He began to feel intoxicated. Dizzy and drunk, bleary and out of balance. The leaves were falling, the golden leaves; the yellow leaves. They were butterflies, they were angels. Brimstones and pale-clouded-yellows, cherubim and seraphim. He could hear the clash of iron on shields, see the flash of swords, the glint of the swinging axes. Toadstools were friars, pushing up from the mould, lifting their tonsures into the light, the splayed and golden light. The jay was an archangel, ethereal and exotic, raucous in the silence, the misted silence. He wandered aimlessly through the falling leaves, the butterflies, the cherubim, the seraphim. Fallen trees were like bodies, dead and decaying bodies. The fungi were eating them, corrupting them. A squirrel was a wave, energy in motion. A vortex, a vortex in the mind of God. Acorns pattered down, spattered like falling blood. It was warm and dank, warm and dank and musky. He could feel the mist on his skin, the tears of Christ; the warm and golden tears of Christ. In the glade he could see the Church of St Nicholas, patron saint of the children, the innocents. Doves were basking under the arches in the Norman tower. The stained-glass windows were rainbows, shimmering and spectral in the golden light. There were ghosts coming out of the mist, out into the glade, the misted grey and sun-shafted glade. Ghosts of kings, ghosts of warriors, ghosts of friars. He was speaking with the ghosts, speaking with the tongues of angels, the tongues of fire. A red rose bloomed in the eerie light. 'Holy Mary mother of God, pray for us sinners now, and at the hour of our death'. The rose held out its hands, its red hands, its blooded hands, It was holding the figure of Christ; the dead Christ, the tortured Christ, the tormented Christ. The mystical rose, the magical rose, the pure and perfect rose.

Was this birth or was it death? He didn't know, he wasn't sure. He walked into the rose; into the Christ, the anointed One. He started to regain composure. The effect of the fly agaric was leaving him, leaving him sane and entirely sensible. Acorns were pattering on the ground. A jay, an exotic jay, was hoarding its winter store. The light was gold; gold and grey, splayed and striated. He walked back into the thickening mist, the silver mist, the shimmering mist. A squirrel was a wave amongst the branches. A silver wave, a nebulous wave; breath on a darkening mirror.

October, and the bees still busy. Pansies and cyclamen, pollen and nectar. They must hoard their sweetness for the winter, the cruel and careless winter. Why was the poet burdened by knowledge, weighted by intellect? Couldn't he become like the bees, no past, no future, only the present, the eternal present? Consciousness he could cope with, but thoughts, the interminable thoughts. A robin was singing, a solitary robin. Wistful and thin was its music, sad and subtle and mournful, soft like the falling leaves. He looked longingly at the bees and the flowers. How could he be as them, thoughtless and in communion? This was St Luke's summer. The atmosphere was mellowed and fruitful, hushed and hallowed. Honey was on his mind. The drink of the Gods, the sweetness of the sun. Was this all serendipity, a chance occurrence, an accident? He didn't think so. There is a design in fragrance, fragrance in design. He smelt deep. Smelt deep into the smells of autumn. The smell of humus, the smell of the late roses, the smell of death and deliverance, love and the promise of spring. Why was he thinking instead of just being. He couldn't stop thinking, thoughts were his life, his *raison d'etre*. If he didn't think then he couldn't write. A dilemma, the horns of a dilemma, the Devil's horns. The sumach was on fire, the roses were on fire. Fire and blood, blood and fire. Heraclitus and Christ. Wine and honey, red and gold. The doves still believed in summer, the collared-doves; the ring-doves. Syllables of sound, syllables of heat, St Luke's heat. Horse-chestnut leaves were green, green and edged with gold, glimmering gold. Their fruits were on the ground, burnished and glistening, brown with a bloom of whiteness at the centre. He picked one up. Held it to his nose. It was a subtle smell, a smell he could not describe. He remembered his youth, the smoke from October fires, the woodsmoke and the decaying humus. The swallows were on the wires, the last swallows, the valedictory swallows. Was he in the past, or the present? He didn't know, he couldn't be certain. Was this time or timelessness? Temporal or eternal? The bees were on the flowers, their long proboscises sipping at sweetness, sipping the drink of the Gods. Were they thinking or just being? Why did he have a past, a present; a projection of the future? Pollen and honey, honey and pollen. Seed and flower, flower and seed. He stood with his back against the trunk of the horse-chestnut tree. He looked up through the leaves, the green and golden leaves. Blue was above him and beyond. Azure and gold, green and gold, gold and viridian. The doves were somnolent and soulful. Syllables of sound, summer sound, ethereal sound, gilded by silence and the fletch of shadows. His thoughts began to leave him. His mind grew wings, veined and diaphanous wings. He lifted above the flowers, hovered and hummed. He was no-one and everyone, nowhere and everywhere. He could taste the nectars, the sweet subconscious nectars. He was in the hive. Everything was dark, dark and yet dazzling with gold. This was his winter store, his warm and thoughtless provisions. He began to dream. Galaxies spun through his mind, intelligible, unintelligible vortices. Circles and spirals; maelstroms and helices. Stars were bees, shimmering velvet bees. Bees in the moon, bees in the sun, bees in the constellations. Death was a shooting star, flaring into the atmosphere, dying of fire, dying of light. He was asleep, not thinking, not dreaming, completely unconscious. His heart was beating slowly, pumping the corpuscles, the corpuscles of the rose; the corpuscles of corn. The Christ and the Virgin hovered above his sleeping head, his blossoming head. They were sipping the sweetness, the sweetness of his thoughtless being. Would he awake, would he ever wake? How could he know, how could he possibly know?

Calm does not exist without the storm, each supposes the other. Calm and storm, love and hate, life and death. Everything has its opposite, its mirror image. It was a calm day in October, calm and sun-shot, yet clouding over. The sea was calm, as calm and as soft as silk. Seagulls were crying, curving and crying in the sky, the azure and yet cloudy sky. A Thames barge was in the doldrums, breathless and becalmed, riding at anchor. The seagulls were flying inland, crying their cries, their harsh and portentous cries. The invisible air was stirred, stirred yet invisible. A prophetic breeze ruffled the silks of the sea, the fathomless silks; the diaphanous silks. Christ was walking on the waters, the rippling waters, the glittering silver waters. The poet was out in his boat fishing for whiting, the large and cod-like channel whiting. The breeze was strengthening, gathering its invisibility, narrowing its invisible isobars. They were raising the sails on the Thames barge, lifting its anchor. It slanted across the rising wind, made for the swatchways and the open sea. The whiting were biting well, one after another came to the waiting gaff. They came from the sea, the deep sea, the fathomless sea. Conscious and subconscious, the depths and the glittering surface. The wind began to gust, claws of wind, scratching the surface, turning the silk to waves. Waves began to crest, rise up and turn over themselves, crash in cacophonous whiteness. Skeins of brent geese were underwriting the sky, the sunlit and clouded sky. Sentences in black ink, long sprawling sentences, thin and wispy and suggestive. Christ was on the water, the glittering water. Christ was in the wind, the bellowing wind, the blustering wind. He decided to make for shore. The weather was closing in; he knew the signs, the portents. He secured his boat to its mooring, loaded the tender, and rowed towards the beach. Water was lapping against the sides, coming over the gunnels. Sea water, violent water, hectic water. He stood on the beach and looked out to sea. The horses were multiplying, galloping horses, white horses, jumping invisible fences. Spume and spray lifted from the glittering surface, filled the air with silver, sunlight and cloud and silver. He chained his tender to the boat rack and made his way home. Christ was in the trees, sunlight and Christ, Christ and the gathering storm. The invisible made visible. It was nearly dusk. The starlings were coming in to roost. Settling and lifting, rising and falling, circling and spiralling. Black photons, black exhausted photons. They reflected the setting sun, the red resplendent sun. Black and red, red and black; rising and falling, circling and settling. They were the sea, the swell of the sea, the rise and fall of the sea. He went indoors; made himself a cup of coffee, filled his pipe, and settled down in front of the garden window. The Gods were angry. The wind was strengthening, building and blowing, blowing and building. Trees, tall strong trees, were bending in the blast, bending and howling, bellowing and blustering. This was the Gods speaking, the angry Gods; the invisible Gods. An oak bent nearly double, held up for an instant, and then was gone. It came crashing into the garden, the writhing and ruinous garden. Its roots were in air, were snakes in the Gorgon's hair, and he was petrified. The sea was in the wind. Crystals of salt, shot-blasted the window-panes, incinerated the cypresses. The invisible was horizontal. Slates and tiles, branches and bits of brick, were hurtling and horizontal, murderous with momentum. His carpet started to lift, curtains and window-panes moved in and out with the pressure, the invisible pressure. He sat in the corner of the room, the pulsating room, listening to the debris falling into the chimney, the howling chimney. He began to hallucinate, or was it an hallucination? The Four Horse-rider's of the Apocalypse hovered in his mind, or was it his room? They were ghostly and ghastly; hooded and heinous, decayed and skeletal. He cried out for his Christ, his Mystical Rose; his golden Dove. The storm began to abate, but he was still trembling, trembling with terror. Was this birth or was this death? He didn't know; he could not be certain. A crucifix swung in his vaulted imagination, or was it his imagination? He was gutting a whiting, a large channel whiting. The viscera were red and gold, gold and viridian. The wind had stopped, all was quiet, quiet and calm and uncanny. He had been awake all night. He opened his front door and looked down the ruinous street towards the sea. The moon-glade was fading with the dawn's first light. Christ was on the waters, the golden and glorious waters. Seagulls were curving across their cries, their harsh, discordant cries. A Thames barge could not find the wind, they lowered the sails and dropped anchor. He walked towards the sea, the silver sea, the glittering sea, the golden sea. Boats had been torn from their moorings, had been blown ashore, were beached and buckled and broken. A flock of starlings circled and spiralled, spiralled and circled, then flew off towards the saltings. Black exhausted photons, forgotten by sunlight, forsaken by sunlight, children of the storm; children of the Apocalypse.

Halloween was upon him, the last day of the Celtic year. The cattle were coming in from the pastures; the sheep were coming down from the hills. Pumpkins with uncanny flickering smiles, apple-bobbing, trick or treat. Time for a feast, a celebration, communion with the ancestors. He remembered St Michael's Church, how as a child he would visit the graveyard on Halloween, how he would tremble in anticipation at the thought of ghosts, witches, warlocks. The full moon was above the hill of St Michael, the Pagan hill, the sacred hill. Were the ghosts in his mind or in the world? He didn't know; he wasn't sure. Jack-o-lanterns skittered across the marshes, lost souls, fallen stars. An owl hooted, a fox barked, and he trembled more violently. Why was he here? What had ghosts got to do with him? He walked widdershins around the church, and out of the air, the misted and moonlit air, the Devil appeared to him. Was it the Devil, was it a dragon or was it a Pagan God? He didn't know; he could not be certain. There was fire certainly, fire and smoke and blood. Passionate blood, fertile blood, ancestral blood. The archangel appeared. The flaming and self righteous archangel. Bolstered by faith; blinded by faith. The dragon belched smoke and fire, but the archangel held his ground, his holy ground, his sacrosanct ground. Was this birth or was it death? He didn't know, how could he know, how could he be certain? St Michael drew his sword, his glittering silver sword. He plunged it into the heart of the dragon, into the heart, into the blood of ages. He had killed the past, murdered the past; defiled the past. Righteous and blind, remorseless and victorious. He would butcher in the Middle-East, strike terror in Jerusalem, the holy city, the city of The Book, the people of The

117

Book. They would be wailing at the wall, wailing in Mecca, wailing in Medina. Torquemada appeared in the mist, the inquisitional mist. The Manichees were murdered, the Cathars were murdered. Hitler appeared in the mist, the Jews were murdered. Stalin was manifest, and the communists were murdered. Where was he, was he in the past, in his childhood? Was he in the future, the endless and intolerable future, the violent and murderous future? How could he know, how could he be certain? There was a knock at the door, he undid the latch, and opened it. "Trick or treat, treat or trick." A golden-haired boy, and a silver-haired girl, stood in the moonlight, the misted and magical moonlight. He gave them apples, golden and silver apples. Apples of the sun, apples of the moon. They smiled, smiled and evanesced, smiled and faded. He was alone, alone at Halloween. The cattle were in from the pastures, the sheep were down from the hills. It was time for a feast, time to speak with the ancestors. But he was alone, alone and trembling, alone and crying. He walked out into the garden, into the moonlight, into the glittering stars. An owl hooted; a fox barked. There was a halo around the moon, an iridescence, a spectral glimmering. A late bat flittered passed on silver wings, on imperceptible threads of sound, silver sound. He was a ghost, the world was a ghost; everything was ghosted. Some golden apples still hung in the misted trees, the shining ones, the illustrious ones. He was in the garden of the Heperides. The daughters of Hesperus were guarding the golden apples; the dragon was guarding the golden apples. A shooting star fell from the heavens like a silver rose, a mystical rose; a magical rose. He held out his arms to the night sky and breathed in deeply. The Virgin was in his heart. The Christ was in his soul. He was crucified by darkness, crucified by light. His garden was the Island of the Blessed; the island of the silver dragon, the island of the golden Christ.

NOVEMBER

John Barleycorn

The fallen pears - ferment: the alcohol
Of autumn - dulls the wasp - and starlings
Stagger sideways: full - content. The wholesomeness

Of summer fills the hedge - where hips and haws
Are claret to the birds - and hops are golden
Goblets: not a pledge. I'm tipsy - with the laws

Of sloes and gin - where drunken tales are told
By every dove - and draughts of wine are stored
Within the grape. This blood - emboldens:

Gives courage to confront the very soul
That summer cloaked in sugars - yeast - and barley.
In veritas - this *vino* - finds the goal -

Where lights intoxication writes the score
That fills the ears of Bacchus: and the glass.

All-Saints; All-Souls. All dead; dead. 9/11 -
11/11/11, insanity, inhumanity, inconceivable.
Rosenberg, Sassoon, Owen: *'Dulce et decorum est
pro patria mori'*. Man was made in God's image.
The image is a hall of mirrors, a distorted image,
God's image distorted. Sometimes comical,
sometimes grotesque. 'Lord have mercy on us,
Christ have mercy on us, Lord have mercy on us'.
The Somme, Ypres, and the fields of Flanders.
Demeter and Persephone. Was it birth or death;
death or birth? He didn't know, he could not be
certain. Hades and Heaven, winter and summer.
Blood and poppies, poppies and blood. Poppies for
remembrance, poppies for summer. 'Goodbye to all
this', all this, all this. Return to the Goddess, the
White Goddess. Live for the Goddess; love the
Goddess. He remembered the fields, the fields
between Ashingdon and Canewdon, the corn
fields, the fields full of poppies. Edmund Ironsides
and Canute, blood and the poppies, death and the
poppies. The blooded hawthorn, his unlucky tree;
the blooded rowan, his lover's tree, the witch's
tree. He stood in his garden. Everything was stark,
stark and cold and leafless. All-Saints; All-Souls.
Time for the ancestors; the holy and the sinners.
Still the robin sang, thin and sad was its song, its
elegy. Here and there a few remaining leaves
flickered in the fitful breeze. Yellow and gold;
gold and red. They fell, one by one, sidled down
the misted air, the cold air. This was too much; the

cuckoos gone, the swifts gone, the swallows a valediction. He began to weep; to cry in the misted air, the frosted air. His tears froze, were crystals on his cheek, falling to the ground, the frozen ground. The robin sang its elegy, and he wept, wept like a little child. He could see St Nicholas's Church in the crystals. Could hear the screams of the Innocents, Herod's laughter, the laughter of the Gods. He had been betrayed, deserted. The moon in the crystals was silver, a handful of silver. Geese flew across the moon, crossed the moon with silver, cried down with the sounds of winter. Was it day or night; summer or winter? How could he know; how could he know? There were poppies in the fields of corn, white poppies; frozen poppies. The river was covered in ice, glittering ice, hot and golden ice. Peewits cried, lifted and curved and dropped. Double notes, repeated phrases, mirror images. He remembered the cuckoo, the duplicity of May, the hawthorn, his unlucky tree, blossoming white, white and hoary in the sight of the lifting sun. What could he do; what could he say? The towers of York, the towers of Nostradamus, they were falling, falling. Crumbling to dust, dust and rubble, rubble and dust. People were crying, screaming, pleading for their lives. The robin would not stop singing, a sad song, a lament, a threnody, a dirge. The mist was elegiac; the cold mist, the frosted mist. 'Holy Mary Mother of God, pray for us sinners now, and at the hour of our death'. He picked up two crystal tears and embedded them deep into his eyes, his azure eyes, his weeping eyes. He could see Elijah, lifting into the sun, burning with the sun. Would he ever come back, would the Christ return, would love return, light return? He didn't know, he couldn't answer. Clouds were beginning to obscure the sky, gather and thicken, chill and condense. The crystals in his eyes began to melt, trickle down his cheeks, his cold and pallid cheeks. They fell into the air, the stark and the cold and the misted air. They were the tears of November rain, God's tears; despondent tears. He closed his eyes, the century's eyes. What could he do; what could he say? A blackbird chinked, like glasses at a wake; and the year's last roses, trembled, then shattered in the drenching silver.

'No sun - no moon - no morn - no noon - no dawn - no dusk - no proper time of day'. He was on the causeway walking out towards Leigh Ray. He was in a bubble of fog, a cold and clinging shroud of invisibility. Waders came into view, whistled and fluted, then disappeared. Was this the way of things, the way of singularity? Was this an approximation of nothingness? Without the waders there was silence, total silence. He stopped walking and the sound of his feet on the pebbles ceased to exist; he had ceased to exist. Was this what it was like, before creation, only potential, possibilities? This was the thought of God. The thoughtless all-knowing; the dazzling darkness. Stars were latent in the fog, waiting in the fog. How could he think in singularity; the eternal? Thinking was a matter of sequence, a consequence of time. How did God think; how could he think? He didn't know, he wasn't sure. A curlew called, the loneliest sound in time, the loneliest sound in the universe. Then again it was silence. Was he alone; was he the only one? Was he God, was it his responsibility, the promises and the possibilities? His skin was goose fleshed, prickle and pimpled, cold and clammy. He could smell the fog, the dank and musky fog. The sun, the pale sun, came in and out of view. The fog was a monstrance; the sun a communion wafer. Darkness suffused with gold, gold diffused into darkness. Was it night or was it day? He didn't know, he couldn't tell. He started to walk again, out towards the Ray, the Leigh Ray. He could hear the sea, the prayer-like sussuration and the whispering waters. He could hear it, but he could not see it. It was invisible; all was invisibility. He could hear the skeins of geese, a cacophony, the baying of dogs; the cry of the hounds of hell. He could hear them, but he could not see them. If heaven exists, then hell exists, at least in the minds of men. All is duality; duality is all. He must transcend it all, the dichotomies and the schisms, all that seems irresolvable. Hitler and Stalin shimmered in the fog, glittered in a sun-

124

shaft. Torquemada was questioning, questioning singularity, questioning the mind of God, the mind of man. The gulls began to scream, scream in the silence - scream in the invisibility. He walked into the Leigh Ray, the glittering Ray; the shimmering Ray. Slowly he submerged, fish swam in and out of his eyes and shore-crabs fastened themselves to his flesh. He was on the rack, he was being tortured. He screamed beneath the waters, the glittering waters. But his scream was silent, as deep as the tide and silent. Nobody heard his screams, no-one was there and nothing existed. Poppies bloomed in the waters, the deep and remembered waters. *'Dulce et decorum est pro patria mori'*. To die for one's country, what country, whose country? He was drowning, drowning in poppies, drowning in blood. 'Holy Mary Mother of God, pray for us sinners now, and at the hour of our death'. He was swallowing blood, swallowing water. He lashed out with his arms and legs, struggled to reach the surface, the glittering surface. Suddenly there was light, the sun's pale wafer shining through the monstrance of the fog. Was this birth or was this death? He didn't know, he wasn't certain. A skein of geese emerged from the looming fog; the nothingness, the singularity. He was beginning to understand. The invisible made visible. Epiphany, biogenesis, creation.

Festivals of fire, rituals of fire. Beltane and Samain, Easter and Pentecost. Pagan fire, holy fire. What does it matter? It's all the same, everything's the same. 'What you see you are'. 'As above, so below'. The cattle are in from the pastures, the sheep are down from the hills. The sacred hills; the Pagan hills. It is time for slaughter, ritual slaughter. The fire has turned to flesh and the flesh will be turned to fire. He remembered the bonfires, the bonfires of his childhood. Why did it always rain, rain when he needed fire, when he needed light? The rain was drenching down, drenching and slanted and silver. The clouds were scudding and sou'westerly, cynical balloons, sullen and inflated, desolate and drenching. Fire had been drowned; the Dove was inundated. He was digging in the garden, turning the earth, the dank earth, the scented earth. Roses were only hips, ghosts of the passing summers. Red hips, mystical hips, passionate hips. He dead-headed the only remaining rose, the tarnished rose, the rose with the tarnished petals. A skylark sang in his mind, in the mist, in the azure, in the gold and the glittering sky. The last chrysanthemums and dahlias seemed funereal, pale and diffuse and funereal. The robin was still singing, mournful and melancholy, a funeral rite, an exequy. Dusk was gathering, the clouds clearing, and the rain beginning to stop. The moon was dilating above the eastern horizon, a red moon, an inflammable moon. Bonfires were being dowsed, dowsed with petrol and soaked with paraffin. Everything was fire; the fire of the moon, the petrol fires, the paraffin fires. The moon was shrinking, shrinking to silver, shrinking to starlight and the thought of frost. His breath was rising like a ghost, an apparition, an epiphany. Rockets roared into the sky on trails of fire. They exploded in the darkness, crackled with fire, cascaded with fire, spectral fire. Bonfires glittered in the frost and the silver moon scattered its powdered ice, its shivering spicules. The night was hoary with frost, golden with fire. The air was dense and heavy. He sat at the garden table in the cold, in the still air, the air that had sunk to zero. The rape fields were golden in his remembering mind. Bees assayed the gold, swifts fathomed the gold. A cuckoo sang and its double notes drifted into the blossom, the may-flowering blossom. Bluebells were fire; indigo flames in the sun-shafts. A yaffle laughed; a great-tit rang its bell. Doves were deliberate with sound, summer sound. His breath was condensing on his moustache and beard. Frost was forming on his face, crystals of frost, spicules of ice. Was this time or was it timeless? He didn't know; how could he be sure? The effigy was burning, decomposing in the flames, dying in the flames. Matthew Hopkins was abroad, the red cloak, the garment of fire, the witch's garment of fire. Torquemada was questioning, the Puritans were questioning, Hitler was questioning. Everything was fire; everything was burning. Heraclitus was at the stake; Heraclitus was in the ovens. The flesh had become fire, the fire was becoming flesh. He got up from the garden table and looked into the moon. The Man in the Moon was crying, the Man in the Moon was laughing. Was this birth or was this death? He didn't know, he wasn't sure. A rocket crashed and cascaded into gold and rainbows. The moon exploded into shards of silver, shimmering silver, glittering silver. He was drenched in silver, showered in silver, drowning in silver. The shards were rose petals, stars, galaxies. The fires were everywhere, the fires were dying; the fires were going out. He opened the door and went into the house. The clock was ticking, ticking, ticking. But he didn't hear it; he didn't know; he could not be certain.

November was coming to an end. All the swallows had gone. The geese had returned. He walked by the river, the cold and misted river. Everything was still, still and inverted in the glass, the fathoming glass. The chiff-chaffs had gone, the warblers had gone. He was alone, alone with the reflections in the river, with the stark trees, the stark and denuded trees. The rooks were rowing across the river, the river of the air. Was this the Styx, was this the meaning, was this all there was? He didn't know; Christ he didn't know! Jackdaws chacked amongst the rooks. Tinny and treble, sharp and metallic. Finches had formed their winter flocks, were gleaning the stubble, the golden stubble. He looked into the glass, scried the glass. A pike was haunting the shallows, long and sinuous and terrible. Shoals of roach were silver seams, unconscious seams, unconscious of endings, unconscious of beginnings. Did the pike know, or was it nothing but instinct, just blind, unthinking carnage? But we know, we all know. 'Lord have mercy, Christ have mercy, Lord have mercy'. Coots and moorhens sullied the icon, shattered the icon. The mist and the glittering water. Crystal and spectra, fish-scales and sunlight. All reflected, all refracted. Leaves were floating on the river, scarlet and golden, viridian and brown. A mosaic, a mosaic in a mosque, a mosaic in a cathedral. The river was stained-glass. Light was the wings of angels, cherubim, seraphim, powers and principalities. A rainbow shimmered in the glass; St Peter shimmered in the glass. He was holding his golden keys, the keys to the kingdom of heaven. The poet reached out but he couldn't hold on to them. Were they iron pyrites, fool's gold - gold in the imagination? He didn't know, he wasn't sure. His confirmation name was Peter. Peter the rock, Peter the fisherman, or Peter as the cock crowed thrice? The water stilled. The sun was in the water. Christ was in the water. Canada geese dragged their clanking chains across the sky. Lines in the sky, words in the sky, prophecies. Moses was in the reeds, a basket of reeds. Moses was in the bushes, the sunlit burning bushes. 'Thou shalt not kill'; 'Thou shalt not kill'. He threw a stone into the river, a carved stone, a commanding stone. Ripples radiated. Concentric circles, circles of life, circles of the seasons, circles of history. Scarlet leaves lifted and fell on the circles, the concentric circles. Were they leaves or were they blood? He didn't know; he could not be certain. Golden leaves glittered on the circles, glittered and shimmered. Were they the golden blood of Christ? The resurrected Christ, the risen Christ? Brown leaves and viridian leaves; Earth and air, fire and water. Four doves alighted in his consciousness. Four doves, four syllabic doves, drowsy and dreamy with the sounds of summer. The water radiated, was a rose, a silver rose, a golden rose. In the centre, the sweet and fragrant centre, a velvet angel sipped at the shimmering nectars, the golden nectars. Was this time or timelessness? How could he know, how could he ever know? A skylark sang in the arc of a rainbow. 'The wise thrush' repeated its summer song. The cuckoo's double note drifted and diminished. He looked at his face, his face in the rippling waters. It was the face of God, the distorted and disfigured face of God. He was in the hall of mirrors, the mirrors of history, the grotesque and distorted mirrors of humanity. The scarlet leaves, the golden leaves. Was it birth or was it death? Blood and the glory of Christ? Blood and the coveted? Blood and the spoils of war? 'This is the blood of the new covenant; drink this in remembrance of me'. The mist was a silver monstrance; the sun a golden wafer. A rising roach, silver and red-finned, shattered the waters surface; hung for an instant in mid-air, crashed back and disintegrated. Dissolved and disappeared.

DECEMBER

Curlews and Oystercatchers

There is a kind of silence that disturbs -
Where moonlight casts its glade across the sea
And chills the mind. A silence that the birds

Will not appease - with sudden bleeps and fluted
Turns of voice - that catch the breeze and drift
Across the tide. Such solitudes are proved

Beyond belief - as midnight brings its gift
Of endless stars - and moves the heart. We lose
Ourselves in universal themes - that shift

The thoughts through littorals of time. No words
It seems could ever bring relief as reason
Dies between the neaps and springs - and stills the verb.

All's motionless along the empty beach
Save where the waves illuminate a curve.

December came in with freezing fog. It was below zero, well below zero. He was with his lover, his soul-mate. They were children of the stars, children of the weather. The trees in the garden were furred with whiteness, looming and luminescent. The fog was grey, grey and azure, azure and gold. Both ponds were frozen solid. White obscuring glass, allowing neither light nor any view, to pass beyond the censor of themselves. This was the weather both he and his lover enjoyed, warmed to, despite the descending mercury. They were children of the ice - ice children. A blackbird fluttered onto the lawn, the frosted lawn, the white and impenetrable lawn. This was the hard time, the cruel time. Yet they loved the frosted trees, the iced ponds, the suffusions of sunlight and the diffusions of azure. All was white and blue and gold. It was the may-flowering thorn. The bluebells and sunlight in its cage of branches. The blackbird was hungry, was cold; was starving. Worms were deep, deep and warm in the musky earth. The blackbird had lost its voice, could only chink, chink like the clash of crystals. But still the robin sang. Exequies, lamentations, dirges. His lover was the Ice Queen and he was the King of Frost. They held hands in the freezing fog, kissed in the cold azure, the glittering gold. The ice dragons had flown from the moon, the centre of the moon, the crystalline heart of the moon. They were both ice and fire. Silver with golden breath; sunlight and moonlight. The dragons walked through the lover's minds, as common as unicorns, as real as the shimmering angels. What could he do; what could they do? They were one with the frost, one with the dragons of ice. A storm-cock tried his voice, but it was frozen, locked in its crystal throat. The world was dying, the garden was dying; everything was dying. But they were in love. In love with each other, in love with the stars, the cold stars, the shivering stars. There was a castle beyond the wind, the north wind. A castle of ice, a glittering castle, a shimmering castle. The castle was made of starlight, they were made of starlight; everything was starlight. Their minds were in the castle and the castle was in their minds. Their hearts were made of ice, their blood was silver and frozen, but they lived; lived in the crystal castle, the glittering silver castle. A flock of starlings flew into the trees. Spicules of ice cascaded into air, glittered and shimmered. The fog was beginning to disperse. The trees were ghosts, ghosts in the azure - ghosts in the realms of gold. The storm-cock found its voice, its crystal throat had melted, and song began to glow, to scintillate. Water surfaced over ice, the ponds were melting and the blackbird was drinking. They were holding hands, looking into each others eyes, azure eyes - golden eyes. A skylark climbed the rungs of Jacob's dream. Dissolved into the sun; disappeared into the sun. A pair of cabbage-whites, coiled and convolved, spun in a double spiral. The lovers walked into the thorn; the may-flowering thorn. A nightingale was serenading, singing a madrigal. There was a scent of sweetness and corruption. Was this birth or was this death? They didn't know, they didn't care. They were holding hands, hands of ice - hands of fire. A unicorn walked amongst the bluebells. A white ethereal unicorn. A song-thrush alighted in the blossom, the white may-flowering blossom. Petals began to fall. Spicules of ice, spicules of sunlight, spicules of song. They merged one into the other, deep into the spheres of song. They were a star, the Pole Star, the white and the wintering star.

He had snow in his heart; whiteness in his soul. Chastity, purity, the perfection of the Virgin, the Goddess. But for him the weather was worsening. Cloud and a warm wind, the westerly wind, the rain-bearing wind. The trees held up arthritic hands in the wind; arthritic and gesticulating. Silver droplets were gathering on their fingers, their gnarled and gesticulating fingers. What were they trying to say? He did not know, he did not have an answer. The clouds were silver balloons, bruised and silver balloons. They scudded across the sky, precursors of the heavier rain to come, the imminent storm. Lapwings and golden plovers ranged across the ploughed fields, the corduroy fields, the glistening fields of clay. Paglesham Church was grey stone in a grey world. Pigeons were hunched and dishevelled along the castellations of the Norman tower. Kentish ragstone. Ragstone from the Middle-Ages. Lord and tenant, serf and master. His mind was a strip of land, his own land, his own and English soil. His consciousness was in the common, in the woods; turbary and pannage, firewood and wild fruits. Small-beer and oxen, oxen and the plough. He walked between the furrows; imagined the ox in front of him. His boots were heavy with clay, thick with clay. The rain was falling, falling at a slant in the wind, falling heavily. Lapwings cried, thin, and shrill, and desolate. The trees were gesticulating in the wind, trying to speak, howling in agony. Christ was in the trees, hung in the trees, nailed to the trees. A battle was fought at Ashingdon, over the brow of the hill, down in the river valley. Edmund Ironsides and Canute, Saxon and Dane. There are poppies in the fields each summer, a gash of poppies, a scar of poppies. St Andrew's Minster, Ashingdon, St Nicholas' Church, Canewdon, St Peters, Pagelsham. Saxon and Norman, cold stone, grey stone. The rain was washing the stone, weathering the stone, eroding the stone. Pigeons flew round in a circle, a spiral, a grey and swirling vortex. Rain spattered into the puddles between the furrows. There was sky in the puddles, silver and bruised clouds, lapwings and plovers. There was snow in his heart; whiteness in his soul. A white blackbird settled in a tree by the headland. Purity, chastity, perfection. Was it a messenger from God, an angel, an annunciation? He didn't know; he could not be sure. The Virgin was in his mind, the Goddess, the mother of God, the lover of God. Parthenogenesis, abiogenesis, creation. A sun-shaft fathomed through a rift in the cloud. A promise, a prophecy, an epiphany. A swallow was caught in the sun-shaft, gilded in the sun-shaft. Was it real or was it imagined? In time or timelessness? How could he know, how could he ever know? A white dove hovered above him clutching a red rose in its bill. A red rose; a mystical rose. There was snow in his heart; whiteness in his soul. Purity, chastity, perfection. There was blood on the snow in his heart, blood on the whiteness of his soul. The rooks were purpled in the sun, purpled and iridescent, purpled and spectral. He stepped onto the headland, kicked the clay from his boots, and began to walk back to his car. He walked passed the lake, under the willows with golden twigs. A moorhen skittered across the surface of the lake. The last sporadic raindrops pitted its velvet meniscus. He got back into his car and turned on the radio. It was a carol service, an early yet welcome singing of the sacred songs. *'Adeste Fideles'*, *'Gloria in Excelsis Deo'*. A raindrop or two trickled down his windscreen; captured the gold in the rifted sunlight. 'Lord have mercy on us,

Christ have mercy on us, Lord have mercy on us'.

Mid December. Neither sun nor rain, snow nor frost. Cloudy and nondescript, neither warm nor cold, wet nor dry. This to his mind was purgatory, limbo. Nothing to say, nothing to be said. Not hell nor heaven, not birth nor death. The world was grey, just grey and brown. Birds had stopped singing. Vegetation was dormant, withered and brown and dormant. The fox was in his lair, the badger was in his den, the hedgehog in his nest of leaves. The hawthorn and rowans the only sign of life. Their red berries, their blooded berries, feeding the redwings and the chattering fieldfares. He had known these fields, these copses, all of his life. Or was it before, or was it after? He didn't know. How could he know? How could he ever know? On his approach the fieldfares exploded from the hawthorn, scattered like living shrapnel. These were the winter fields, the killing fields, the wired and trenched, inconceivable fields. He could see the corpses, the blooded and mutilated corpses. Intestines had spilled out and the rats were devouring them. *'Dulce et decorum est pro patria mori'*. The hawthorn had bloomed with poppies; the rowan had bloomed with poppies. 'At the going down of the sun and in the morning we will remember them'. 'They will not grow old as we grow old'. 'Holy Mary Mother of God pray for us sinners now, and at the hour of our death'. In the distance was the sea, the northern sea, the grey eternal sea. Seagulls followed the plough, the late plough, turning the furrows, the shining furrows. The ploughboy is dead, the bird-scarers are dead and the lost and the lonely sweethearts are dead. Brent geese were coming in from the sea, settling on the winter wheat, the green and welcome flush of winter wheat. They lifted and circled, circled and spiralled. Vortices of sound, cacophonies of sound. Were these the hounds of hell? Was hell anywhere else? Was this not Hades, the smokes and the fumes of Hades? It must be, where else but the world of men, the horrors of incarnation, the weakness of the flesh, the poverty of spirit? Winter was too much for him, it was becoming unbearable. It was the winter of his soul, the world's soul, the soul of history. Was this time or timelessness? Birth or death? Genesis or Revelations? How could he know? Does the Goddess know? Does God know? He lay face down in the mud. Shells were exploding all around him. He was covered in earth, in blood, in the blasted flesh of a thousand histories. He sank into the mud, deep into the mud. 'I am the resurrection and the life, saith the Lord: he that believeth in me, though he were dead, yet shall he live: and whosoever liveth and believeth in me shall never die'. He was deep in the mud; deep in the clinging mud. His heart was beating slowly like a rose: a red rose, a silver rose, a white rose, a golden rose.

Poppies grew out of his eyes, budded and blossomed, died and returned their seed. He lay in the dank, the dank and the dreadful darkness, listening to his breath, his faltering breath. He could smell the earth, feel the earth - taste the earth. 'From clay we came, to clay we will return'. 'Ashes to ashes, dust to dust'. *In nomine Patris, et filii, et Spiritus Sancti,* Amen.

It was nearly the winter solstice, nearly Christmas. The sun would stand still; stand still for three days, a trinity of days. Along his street many of the houses had been decorated. White lights, coloured lights, images of reindeers, snowmen, Father Christmases. Christmas trees glinted and gleamed out of the festive windows. He liked to walk along the Broadway during Advent. Beneath the garlanded lights, the budding lights, the blossoming lights in the mid-winter darkness. A Salvation Army Band stood under the lamplight on a street corner. Their instruments glittered in the cold and frosted air. Gold and silver; silver and gold. Could this be the reflection off the wings of angels; the shining ones, the glorious ones? He didn't know, but it could be true, surely it could be true. The carols drifted in the lamplight, in the glare of a gleaming and towering conifer. Which were the stars in the firmament, and which were the Christmas bulbs? Golden lights, azure lights, viridian lights, red lights, starlight and illuminations. Everything was spectral, everything glimmered - everything glittered. Frost was glittering on the grass, white and reflective, shimmering crystals. The shop windows splayed light into the December darkness, into the once severe and sombre streets. Hot chestnuts were being roasted. Hot potatoes eaten, eaten and dripping with molten butter. He walked into the church, the dark and candle-lit church. He knelt at the altar and began to pray. He prayed like he had never prayed before. Christ is it true? Holy Mary Mother of God is it true? God of God, Very God is it true? He didn't know, he still wasn't certain. He had faith but his faith had been tested, sorely tested. He could smell the incense of his youth, hear the hand bells being rung - hear the choirs and the plainsong. He was drifting back, back into the past, the Medieval past, back to a time before the dissolution. The Gregorian Chanting rang out in his remembering mind, his monastic mind. *'Dominus vobiscum - et cum spiritu tuo'*. He was in his cell, the cell of his remembering mind. Was it time or timelessness? Was it then or was it now? He didn't know, he didn't care; it didn't matter. He stood up, genuflected, and made the sign of the cross. He walked along the centre aisle of the nave, between the lighted candles, and the glimmering stations of the cross. The silver cross, the flaming silver cross. He walked out into the festive streets, turned up the collar on his coat, blew his warm and

By the same author:

Poetry

Two Essex Poets (with Frederic Vanson) -
Brentham Press
Talking to the Bees - Brentham Press
Autumn Manuscript - Littoral Press
The Beatitudes of Silence - Littoral Press
Double Vision (with Clare Harvey) - Littoral Press

Autobiography

The Willow Pond - Littoral Press
The Incomplete Dangler - Littoral Press

General

Reflections (The Chelmer & Blackwater
Navigation) - Littoral Press

Other books by the Littoral Press:

Poetry

Fields of Asphodel - Mary Blake
Everyday Objects and Chance Remarks - Derek
Adams